Contents

The Road to Freedom

A story from the life of Moses

I suppose if this had been the Wild West there would have been a 'Wanted!' poster with his name on it. But this was Egypt, more than two thousand years before the printing press . . . although that didn't alter the fact that he was a wanted man. A fugitive. A criminal on the run.

His name was Moses and the charge against him was murder. If they ever caught up with him, he'd be a dead man. The only thing he could do was to lie low for a while till the heat died down – and so he slipped quietly across the border into Midian, and merged into the background.

It was a humiliating experience for a man like Moses, for he was no run-of-the-mill cut-throat, no trained killer . . . He was, in fact, a prince; a man with money and power – a man used to fine clothes in his wardrobe and clean sheets on his bed; a man respected in the house of Pharaoh, the ruler of Egypt.

But although he was nobility, Moses was not an Egyptian. He was an Israelite, and he held his privileged position because he had been adopted by one of Pharaoh's daughters when he was a baby. As her 'son', he had grown up surrounded by all the benefits and trimmings which go hand-in-hand with royalty. Yet Moses could not forget the fact that the blood which pulsed through his veins was Israelite blood . . . and it was this fact which led him to take another man's life.

Population explosion

At that time the Israelites were slaves to the Egyptians. Many years before, the two peoples had lived side by side, but when the Israelite population 'exploded', the Egyptians began to panic. They were frightened that their allies would soon outnumber them. If a war broke out, Israel might side with Egypt's enemies – and that would be fatal.

'Nip it in the bud,' said Pharaoh. 'That's what we'll do! We won't give them a *chance* to overpower us – we'll make them our servants *now*, while we can still contain them!'

And that's what they did. They stripped the Israelites' homes of every comfort, took whips to their backs, and set them to work in the filthy, back-breaking brick-fields. Humiliation? That was only the beginning of it . . .

Murder

Moses knew how badly his people were being treated, but there was nothing he could do about it. After all,

he was no fool. He wasn't going to storm into Pharaoh's office and tell him to lay off the Israelites. If he did he might find *himself* sweating like a pig, mixing clay and straw all day down at the brick-fields. No, on an official level, Moses seemed to have washed his hands of his people . . . but inside, his temper was on the boil, ready to explode. And one day it did.

He had wandered down to the brickworks to look up a few of his Israelite friends when he came across an ugly scene. One of the Egyptian supervisors, whose job it was to see that the Israelites got on with their work, was beating up one of the Israelite workers. Before long the man was writhing in the dust, clasping his gashed head and whimpering in pain.

This was too much for Moses. Looking about to see that he wasn't being watched, he charged in, fists flying . . . and before he knew it the Egyptian was lifeless, sprawled awkwardly on the ground. Quickly Moses dug a shallow grave and rolled the body in, thinking that no one would ever know.

But somebody knew, and somebody told . . . and Moses was a wanted man.

Other plans

Midian seemed a good place to hole up. The chances were that the Egyptians wouldn't think of looking for him here, hundreds of miles the other side of the border. If he were fortunate – and careful – he could remain free. It just meant steering well clear of Egypt. And that, he thought, he could manage very well.

But then Moses had reckoned without God. And God had other plans . . .

It was some years later when God's plans came to light. Moses had married by then, had a family, and settled down to a steady job as herdsman for Jethro, his father-in-law.

It began one morning when Moses was out with his flocks in the rough scrubland near Mount Horeb, that awe-inspiring giant of the Sinai desert. Looking around, his attention was suddenly caught by a bush on fire – not an uncommon sight in that sun-scorched, tinder-dry land. But there was something very strange about this bush. It was blazing fiercely, yet it was not eaten up by the flames.

Puzzled, Moses went to investigate. But before he

could get much closer a voice called out to him: 'Moses, Moses . . .' It was the voice of God.

Holy ground

The herdsman was stunned. There was no one to be seen.

'Who – who are you?' he stuttered.

'Stop where you are,' said the voice. 'Take off your shoes, for you're on holy ground. I am your God – the God of your people's forefathers, Abraham, Isaac and Jacob . . .'

Immediately Moses dropped his staff and clasped his hands to his eyes, afraid to look in case he saw God himself – for to look on God's face meant instant death.

Nervously Moses listened as God explained that the Israelites had cried to him to release them from their slavery in Egypt.

'I have seen their sorrows and heard their cries,' said God, 'and I am going to deliver them and lead them into a rich and fertile land of their own – the land of Canaan – just as I promised their fore-fathers. And you, Moses, are going to lead them. You will go to Pharaoh and demand that he lets my people go!'

Moses' knees turned to jelly. 'B-but I can't do that! You've got the wrong man . . .'

Moses had yet to learn that God never makes mistakes.

'I will be with you,' God assured him, 'and the Israelite leaders will accept you as my ambassador. They will go with you to Pharaoh, the king of Egypt. Together you will tell him that I have met with you and told you to go three days' journey into the desert to worship me there.

'But,' warned God, 'I know that he *won't* willingly let you go. Pharaoh is so stubborn that I shall have to

put great pressure on him to release you. All Egypt will suffer terrible things because of him. But *then* he will free you . . .'

'Send someone else!'

'P-please,' Moses protested, 'I'm no speaker! I've never been good with words – and besides, I've a speech impediment . . .'

'Who made your mouth?' demanded God. 'Didn' *I*? You do as I tell you – I'll see to it that you speak well. I'll even tell you what to say!'

But Moses would not be comforted. 'Please, Lord, he begged, 'send someone else!'

At this God became angry. 'Very well – your brother Aaron is an eloquent man . . . I will send him with you; you will tell him what to say and he will be your spokesman.'

In all the excitement, Moses had almost forgotten the main reason why he didn't want to show his face in Egypt again. He was still a criminal – and prob-ably still on the 'wanted' list. But God told him, 'Don't be afraid about returning to Egypt. All the people who were after your blood are now dead.'

And with that reassurance, Moses packed his travelling bag, put his wife and sons on a donkey, and set out for Egypt.

A week to worship

If the Israelite brick-workers had had a trade union, Moses and Aaron would have been the shop stewards.

They strode into Pharaoh's office that morning as if they had come to negotiate with the management for a holiday for the workers.

'God has spoken to us,' said Aaron, putting the case. 'Give us a week off to go and worship him in the desert.'

'So that's it, is it?' snapped Pharaoh indignantly. 'And just who is your God that I should pay any attention to this nonsense? You certainly cannot have time off!'

Moses and Aaron persisted. 'We *must* obey our God,' they said firmly.

'Look, just who do you think you are?' stormed Pharaoh. 'Troublemakers – that's what you are! Trying to disrupt production! Get back to your work at once!'

The management was already working a very tough productivity deal with the brick-workers: they had to produce so many bricks per day, and in return they didn't get whipped. Now that deal was made even harsher. Pharaoh issued a new directive to the Egyptian supervisors: 'Up till now the Israelites have been provided with the materials for making the bricks. As from today they will collect their own materials – but they must *still* produce the same number of bricks!'

Curses

When word of this reached the Israelites, they were livid. Their foremen immediately went to plead with Pharaoh. 'We just can't keep up the same output as before,' they cried.

'Oh yes you can,' said Pharaoh. 'Obviously you don't have enough work, otherwise you wouldn't be asking for time off to go and worship your God. Now get back to your jobs!'

As the foremen left the building, Moses and Aaron were there, waiting. Had the talks broken down? The look on the men's faces told its own story. They pushed past Moses and Aaron, cursing them.

'Thanks to you two the men's lives have been made hell. If ever the Egyptians needed an excuse to kill us, *you've* given it to them!'

Moses was utterly baffled and disappointed, and hurried away to plead with God.

'Lord,' he cried, 'how could you let such a thing happen? I gave Pharaoh your message – but all he's done is to treat your people even more brutally! Why, you haven't delivered them at all!'

But the Lord answered: 'Now you will see what I shall do to Pharaoh . . . I will prove to all the Egyptians that I am God. In the end Pharaoh will not only let my people go – he will actually be glad to see the back of them.

'Tell the people of Israel that by mighty power and great miracles I will set them free. I promised them the land of Canaan – and Canaan *shall* be theirs.'

Some sort of miracle

Moses and Aaron were dreading their next audience with Pharaoh. They had, after all, been turfed out of the palace once already. But this next visit revealed a more reasonable side of Pharaoh's character. He was now willing, it seemed, to give their request more tolerant consideration. But there was a condition: first they had to prove that their God had sent them by performing some sort of miracle. God, of course, knew this would happen and had already told them what to do to prove their authority.

As Pharaoh looked on, Aaron threw down his staff – and as it struck the floor it became a snake! The ruler was unmoved. At the snap of his fingers, the office doors swung open and in stepped a group of men, each bearing a staff. These were Pharaoh's sorcerers – men who practised magical arts and illusions. At their master's command they threw down their staffs, and these too turned into snakes.

Pharaoh looked smugly at Moses and Aaron, as if to say, 'So much for your miracle!'

But then Aaron's snake suddenly attacked and swallowed up the other snakes! Yet even this would not make Pharaoh listen.

By now Moses was convinced that Pharaoh would not willingly release the Israelites. God would have to show his strength in an undeniable way before Pharaoh would give in. The pressures brought to bear on the Egyptians would be many and severe . . . and they would begin the next morning.

River of blood

As Pharaoh and his entourage came down to the River Nile next morning, Moses and Aaron were

there to meet him. Grim-faced, Aaron stepped forward.

'Because you wouldn't listen before, Pharaoh,' said Aaron sternly, 'the Lord God says, "Now you are going to find out that I am God . . . Moses will hit the waters of the Nile with his rod – and the river shall turn to blood! The fish will die, the river will stink, and no one will be able to drink its waters!" '

Then Moses struck the river with his rod. Immediately the water turned blood-red – and the smell was terrible!

But then Pharaoh's sorcerers appeared, and with their tricks showed that they could do the same. So Pharaoh would not believe . . . and would not let the Israelites go.

A week later, Moses and Aaron went again to confront Pharaoh. 'Our God,' they announced, 'says, "Release my people so that they may worship me. Refuse and I will fill your land with frogs. The Nile will be choked with frogs, and the whole land will be plagued with them . . ." '

But Pharaoh refused and the frogs appeared. They swarmed over the countryside until the creatures were everywhere. They filled the pots and pans in the Egyptians' kitchens. They got into the palace. And there were even frogs in Pharaoh's own bed!

The sorcerers, determined to prove that this was not the work of God, also caused frogs to appear.

But this only made things worse. No one could ge rid of them!

Finally, knee-deep in frogs, and feeling quite des perate, Pharaoh summoned Moses and Aaron.

'Please, please,' he begged, 'plead with your God t banish these wretched creatures – then I'll let you people go and worship.'

So Moses prayed, and the frogs were destroyed But Pharaoh, when he saw that all the frogs were gone changed his mind.

'No,' he said, 'I will *not* let the people go!'

Series of disasters

So God sent a plague of lice throughout Egypt. The covered the animals and they covered the people until the entire land was infested.

The sorcerers, so cock-sure of their magic, said they too could make lice appear. But they tried – and failed.

Helpless and powerless, they turned to Pharaoh 'This is the hand of God!' they declared. Bu Pharaoh's heart was hard. He would not listen. He would not listen, it appeared, *whatever* steps God took against Egypt. Swarms of flies were sent to cover the land . . . a fatal disease swept through the Egyptians' livestock . . . ugly, painful boils broke out on men and animals alike . . . a terrifying storm broke over the land, with thunder, lightning and great hail stones smashing down everything in their path . . . locusts came out of the sky – so many that they blotted out the sun – and ravaged the land, devouring every leaf and ear of corn which had survived the storm . . . darkness descended upon Egypt for three days, preventing the Egyptians from moving about or preparing food . . .

All these disasters struck Egypt in the space of one

ear. The country's industry was wrecked, its agriculture almost ruined, and its economy collapsed. To
make the lesson even more pointed, the land of
Goshen, where the Israelites lived, suffered none of
these hardships.

But Pharaoh – as God had said – still would not
yield.

God's instructions

Finally, God told Moses, 'I will send one more
disaster on Egypt, and after that Pharaoh will practi-
cally kick you out of the country. For tonight, at
midnight, I will pass through Egypt and the eldest
child in every family shall die . . .'

This time, however, the Israelites would only be
exempt if each family followed God's instructions.
A lamb was to be killed and its blood daubed on the
posts and lintel framing every family's front door.
When God passed over, he would look for this sign –
and leave unharmed every family that had done as he
had told them. (From that day to this, the nation of
Israel has commemorated the night of the Passover –
that night of death, when God spared the eldest sons
of the families of Israel.)

As for the Egyptians, that night was one of the
blackest in their history. There wasn't a home in the
land where death did not strike. Even in Pharaoh's
palace there was grief and mourning as the king's
eldest boy lay dead.

Pharaoh could hold out no longer. His will was
broken, his spirit crushed. In the middle of the
night he sent for Moses and Aaron.

'Leave us!' he ordered. 'Take your people and your
animals and go. Get out of my sight! I don't ever
want to set eyes on you again! Now be gone!'

Independence

The Israelites didn't need to be told twice. That
very night, under the direction of their great leader,
Moses, they threw their bags over their shoulders,
rounded up their herds, and headed out of Egypt. Six
hundred thousand men, let alone women and children – and that was some procession.

As they went they laughed and chatted and sang.
Well, why not? This was their night of independence;
a night for rejoicing; a time for celebration. They
had been delivered. God had set them free.

'But of course!' grinned an old man. 'Our God
always keeps his promises!'

'I'll believe that when we reach Canaan!' scoffed
one of the younger men. 'Getting out of Egypt's one
thing . . . possessing the promised land – well, that's
another matter!'

'Patience . . .' said the old man.

And they were going to need it. Canaan was
another forty years away. But they would get there.

God had promised it . . .

Moses/**Fact-finder**

Bible passage

You will find this story about Moses in Exodus 2 – 12. The crossing of the Red Sea, Moses' next adventure, comes in Exodus 12 and 14 (retold in *Great Adventures of the Bible*). You can read more about the life of Moses in the rest of Exodus and Numbers. Deuteronomy records his final words to the nation of Israel, and his death.

Time

The events took place about 1270 BC.

Setting of the story in history

The escape from Egypt took place nearly 400 years after the people of Israel had first settled there. (See the story of Joseph in *Great Adventures of the Bible*.) Joseph had been dead nearly 300 years. During this time the Egyptians rose up and overthrew the hated foreign Hyksos ('shepherd') pharaohs who had known Joseph. Egypt grew great again under a new dynasty of rulers. They were determined never again to be surprised by enemy attack. They built a chain of forts on the Suez frontier. And they sent their armies across the border to crush the tribes of Canaan, marching right up to the north of Syria.

Then they turned their attention to the Israelites. These foreigners with their flocks and herds had flourished in fertile Goshen since Joseph's day. There were enough of them now to pose a real threat, if they turned nasty. So Pharaoh made slaves of them, setting them to hard labour. And he gave his soldiers orders to kill every boy baby at birth. But God had not forgotten his people. He had other plans.

In Pharaoh's court

Thanks to his resourceful mother, Moses escaped death as a baby, and was brought up instead by a daughter of Pharaoh himself (you can read the story in Exodus 1:8 – 2:10). In one of Pharaoh's harems Moses was taught to read and write in the Egyptian scripts. He learnt to fish and hunt. He was trained in archery and warfare, and

for responsibility in the state. He was not the only foreigner to reach a high position amongst Pharaoh's officials.

The Pharaoh Moses had dealings with was most probably Ramesses II. We know that he sponsored a great building programme in the Nile Delta area where the Israelites lived. Although his people regarded him as a god, he was not remote and made a point of hearing their requests in person.

Life under the Pharaohs was good for those who were well off. Here a nobleman with his wife and daughter enjoy a day's wild-fowling from a reed boat in the marshes. His hunting-cat has caught a bird.

Granite statue of Ramesses II. The sacred snake decorating his helmet leads him to victory. In his hand is a crook, his royal sceptre and symbol of authority.

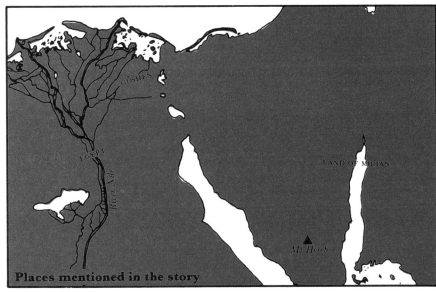

Places mentioned in the story

The plagues

The first nine plagues are what might be called 'natural' disasters. These things (or similar ones) have been known to happen in Egypt – but never one after another like this in the space of a year. And never announced beforehand, as God announced them here, warning of what would happen if Pharaoh refused to listen. The Egyptians worshipped nature-gods. These nine disasters show how powerless these 'gods' were. God is the one who is in absolute control of his creation. The last terrible disaster has no parallel in history.

God does not enjoy destruction. How could he? After all he *made* the people and the cattle and the land. He does not show off his power simply for kicks. He gave Pharaoh good warning and ample opportunity to change his mind. (If you read the story in the Bible you will find that after a time some of the people took notice of God's warnings, and escaped the disasters.) But Egypt's obstinate ruler – the man who thought himself god – deliberately challenged the real God. The responsibility for what followed rests firmly on his shoulders.

The desert locust develops rapidly from wingless, hopping larvae to the winged adults that migrate in swarms carried by the wind. They consume every green thing in their path, and are themselves edible.

Brick-making

The Israelites were forced to produce bricks for Pharaoh's great building projects. The bricks were made of mud, sand and chopped straw, mixed together with water. They were placed in open wooden moulds in long rows and left to bake in the hot sun. Sometimes they were stamped with Pharaoh's name, or the name of the building they were used for – a new palace, or a store-city, or a tomb.

War of Nerves

A story of Joshua

I do want you to know that I'm not doing this for the money. It's true that the newspapers offered me a tidy sum for my story, but they're only after sensationalism and I told them where to go. Besides, they only came to me because my sister Rahab turned them down. She'd told us straight that we weren't to give interviews to scandal-hunters. And seeing that it's thanks to her the family escaped death at Jericho, I reckon I owe it to her to keep my mouth shut. On the other hand . . . well, I'll be honest – I like the look of you, and I think you're only interested in what really happened. But for goodness' sake don't let Rahab hear about this. For a woman she packs a pretty powerful punch. She used to run an inn in Jericho, and you should have seen her in action! A woman in her line of business needs to be able to look after herself. And quite a few drunks in the city would have testified that she certainly could!

Deeds of daring

It's no secret that, as well as running the inn, my sister was a prostitute. (I'm not defending or accusing her – just giving you the facts.) But ask anyone now and they'll tell you she's abandoned all that for the sake of the God who delivered us – and Joshua, Israel's leader.

Of course, it's Joshua you really want to hear about. Well, now that I've met him I know that he's a normal human being. A brave soldier, a wise statesman, and a devoted follower of his God – but not superhuman. Maybe that doesn't surprise you. But time was when the inhabitants of Jericho thought he was anything *but* an ordinary mortal.

Over the years we'd heard plenty of tales of Joshua's deeds of daring and courage as a young warrior under Moses. He was an expert fighter who'd become something of a living legend to the Israelites. But to us in Jericho he was a living nightmare! A giant. A superman. To his enemies he was walking death. And Jericho was in his path.

Challenge

I'm no military strategist, but I knew that when the Israelites decided to cross into Canaan it would be near Jericho. The city guarded the entrance to central Canaan; what you might call the gateway to the promised land. So it was an obvious challenge to the Israelites. If they were to possess Canaan they must first conquer Jericho.

But Joshua had been camped at Shittim, a few miles the other side of the Jordan, for quite a while. The optimists said this meant that the Israelites had decided after all to settle down there. But the truth of the matter was that they were still recovering from the death of Moses, the man who had led them out of slavery in Egypt and been their leader for over forty years. He died within striking distance of Canaan. There was a month's official mourning, and after that the Israelites had to get used to life under their new leader.

Personally I reckoned that, no matter how long he took to act, sooner or later Joshua would be coming over that river. And when the spies arrived at the inn that night my suspicions were confirmed.

Escape route

They'd been sent, as you can guess, to reconnoitre our military strength, and to test the morale of the citizens. They'd come to the right place of course. The inn, I have to admit, was not the most respectable establishment in Jericho. There was always some dark corner where information could be begged, bought or blackmailed from someone. And if none of these methods was successful there were plenty of back alleys where less co-operative subjects could be 'persuaded' to part with their knowledge.

However, such measures weren't necessary for Joshua's spies. The facts they were after were to be had just by keeping their ears open. The threat of an Israelite attack, and the city's ability to repel it, was the main topic of conversation at every table. It had been so ever since we'd first had word of Joshua's arrival at Shittim.

Now don't ask me how, but Rahab knew that these two fellows were Israelites the moment they walked through the door. I suppose if *I'd* realized it I would have had a go at them, or called the police – or kicked up a rumpus. But not my sister. She's a shrewd one. She'd already made up her mind that, because they had such a great God, the Israelites would take Jericho. And she saw the spies as a means of saving our family.

But one of the customers also suspected the men were enemy spies – and *he* saw them as a means of lining his pocket from the king's purse.

Treason?

By the time the police arrived it was nearly closing time and most of the customers had left.

'Where are those two strangers?' the police wanted to know. 'We've reason to believe that they're Israelite spies.'

'Spies?!' said Rahab, pretending to be surprised. 'I didn't know they were spies! They left as the city gates were closing for the night. If you go after them now I expect you'll catch them before they reach the Jordan.'

But the police would never have caught them outside the city – for they were still inside, hiding on the roof of Rahab's house, above the inn!

Now I know you're going to question the ethics of what she did. I suppose that in a court of law she could have been tried for treason. But, as I said earlier, Rahab was convinced that Jericho would fall to the Israelites because their all-powerful God had decreed it. So, even if she had turned over the spies to the police, Joshua would still have taken the city. But that's by the way.

Victory secure

In exchange for harbouring the spies, Rahab asked that when the city was attacked she and our family might be spared.

'It's a deal,' said the spies. 'But when we attack you must have this red rope hanging out of your window so that our armies will be able to identify your house and leave you unharmed. So long as you and your family stay inside the house you'll be safe.'

Then the two men slipped out of the window and climbed down the rope to the ground – for Rahab's house was built on the city wall.

At Rahab's suggestion the spies didn't attempt to head back to Shittim straight away, because the countryside was swarming with security forces out for their blood. Instead they hid in the mountains for a few days, returning to the Israelite camp when the search had been called off.

When they finally made their report to Joshua he knew that victory was secure.

'The people over there have heard of all the great

things our God has done for us,' they said, 'and they're scared stiff. Rahab, the woman who helped us escape, says that even the *name* Israel strikes terror into people's hearts. There's no doubt about it – the Lord is going to give us the entire land.'

Next morning the Israelites broke camp and set out for the Jordan River.

Fool's dream

If anybody needed convincing that Joshua was a great leader – and that his God was the supreme God – the next few days were to provide all the evidence they could want.

On the face of it, conquering Jericho was a foo[l] dream. The city itself was a well-known stronghol[d] a fortress that was the last word in security. It ha[s] withstood enemy sieges over thousands of years. Sure[ly] it wasn't likely to fall now to this rabble of foot-so[re] nomads? Why, Jericho had defeated greater armi[es] than this more times than it could remember!

But if you'd told that to the quaking citizens [of] Jericho that morning they would simply have tol[d] you that other armies hadn't had the God of heave[n] fighting for them.

Then what about the river? It was spring. Th[e] mountain snows were melting, and the Jordan ha[d] overflowed its banks all the way to the Salt Se[a.] Nobody in his right mind tried to cross that ragin[g] torrent at this time of year. The spies had manage[d] it, but one of the reasons they had been chosen wa[s] because they were strong swimmers. How man[y] strong swimmers were there in Joshua's army?

But not even that thought comforted the inhabitan[ts] of Jericho. Hadn't Israel's God opened up the Re[d] Sea so that the people could cross on dry land? H[ad]

wasn't likely to let anything so trivial as a river stop him!

In spirit, the people of Jericho were already dead.

Mighty leader

But what of the Israelites? Were they as sure of victory as we were of defeat?

Well, I think it's fair to say that they were only as sure as Joshua's faith was strong. You see, Joshua wasn't only their military commander; he was their heart. If their heart told them to do something, they knew they could do it. And their heart, on this occasion, was telling them to cross the River Jordan and to capture Jericho.

To my mind this is what made Joshua such a mighty leader: he was prepared to obey God *regardless*. I suppose you'd call it blind faith. You have to admire it. Jordan's greedy currents could swallow a man in seconds. Joshua realized that. But it made no difference to his action. God had told him to take the people across. His duty, as he saw it, was to step into the river. It was up to God to deal with the water.

You don't believe it? Listen, from the walls of Jericho you could get a good view across the plain to the Jordan. I *saw* that river dry up with my own eyes. The Israelite priests who were carrying the ark (a sort of wooden chest – the sign that their God was present with them) stepped into the water, and from that moment it began to go down.

Unnerving sight

Later I learned what happened. Some miles upstream, at the city of Adam, the river was suddenly dammed and the water began to pile up. Below the point of the blockage the water flowed on till it ran into the Salt Sea, leaving the riverbed empty. While the priests stood with the ark on dry ground in the middle, the Israelites crossed over. A more unnerving sight I've yet to see.

Hours later, when everyone was safely across, Joshua ordered the priests to come up out of the riverbed – and the second they set foot on the bank, the dam at Adam broke and the Jordan flowed again.

I suppose this incident was a sort of turning-point in the Israelite invasion. From that day on Joshua's authority was unquestioned. And when the nations west of the Jordan heard how the Israelites had crossed the river on dry ground, their courage drained away and they were gripped with fear. They had good cause to be. Joshua was coming their way.

War of nerves

For those of us in Jericho the nail-biting began when Joshua set up camp in Gilgal, not much more than a mile away. There was no doubt about his intentions now. Even the optimists had surrendered to the inevitable. But what nobody knew was *how* the enemy would attack. From that moment on we manned the walls day and night. Jericho was ready for them.

But the Israelites, I discovered later, weren't ready for us! For the time being they let us stew in our own juice – while they, in their cock-sure manner, took time off for religious ceremonies and feasts.

This was turning into a war of nerves.

Yet little did we realize that Joshua had an even better reason for delaying the siege . . . He hadn't yet

'How long are they going to keep this up?' growled the Captain of the Guard. The answer was: not very long. The column completed one circuit of the city, then peeled off and headed back to their base.

But they were back again next morning. And the next. And the – well, they marched round Jericho once a day for six days! By then it seemed that they intended to keep up the ritual until we surrendered out of sheer frustration.

But the crunch was coming.

Miracle!

On the seventh day the Israelites marched round Jericho *seven* times! And as they completed the seventh circuit the priests blew one long blast on their trumpets.

'Shout!' yelled Joshua. 'God has given us the city!'

And all the people shouted at the tops of their voices!

That was startling enough. But even more terrifying was the movement of the walls. Right round the city the walls, from the foundations up, began to shudder – and before we knew it they were crashing down all around!

Believe me, at that moment Rahab's house was just about the most dangerous place to be. The vibrations rocked the walls, floors and ceilings – and we all thought we were done for. But by some miracle – and it must have been a miracle – the stretch of wall on which the house was built remained standing. We were safe after all!

But it was a different story for the rest of Jericho. No sooner had the last stone fallen than the armies of Israel came charging over the ruins, yelling their threats and waving their swords . . .

Some say that that's when the battle of Jericho really began. But the truth is, it had already ended. For by this time there wasn't a man in the city with an ounce of fight left in him!

First bold steps . . .

Needless to say, it was all over very quickly. But not before we'd had our fair share of scarey moments wondering whether the spies would remember their promise to us. The red rope still hung from the window, as it had done throughout the siege. But would they remember . . . ?

Well, the fact that I'm alive to tell you my story proves that they hadn't forgotten us. They sought us out personally and conducted us safely from the city. They even gave us a couple of tents to live in. And later on the Israelites adopted us into their own family, where we've remained to this day.

And that's it. That is how the Israelites took Jericho, *and* took their first bold steps into the promised land.

Now I know some will say that it all sounds a bit of a tall story. But you can take it or leave it. I was there, so I know. All that I've told you really did happen. And I've got a mother, father, brother, sister and two grannies who'll bear me out.

But listen, would I lie to you? Like I said, I'm not doing this for the money . . .

any idea of how he was going to take the city. He was waiting for orders from God!

They arrived a few days later. Joshua was sizing up the city when suddenly he was confronted by a man with a sword in his hand.

'Friend or foe?' challenged Joshua.

'I am commander of the Lord's army!' was the reply.

Immediately Israel's leader fell to the ground in worship.

'Please, give me your orders.'

Troops and trumpets

We in the city discovered what those orders were at dawn next morning. And we couldn't believe our eyes! The Israelites were marching all round the walls!

The army led the way. Behind them came the priests, carrying the ark and blowing ram's-horn trumpets. And these were followed up at the rear by a smaller detachment of troops. None of the soldiers spoke . . . none brandished a sword . . . and no attempt was made to enter the city. And yet it *was* an assault of a kind. An attack on our nerves; a blow to our minds. I can only say that it was . . . eerie. Disturbing. Undermining.

Joshua/ **Fact-finder**

Bible passage

You will find this story about Joshua in Joshua 2 – 6. Deuteronomy 34 and Joshua 1 tell how Moses died and Joshua became leader of the nation of Israel in his place. Joshua 7 – 24 tells the rest of the story of this great man.

Time

About 1230 BC.

Setting of the story in history

The people of Israel left Egypt in about 1270 BC. Because of their disobedience, God condemned them to live as nomads in the 'wilderness' (the desert/steppe country of Sinai) for 40 years. Not even Moses was allowed to enter the 'promised land' of Canaan. Moses died; the people mourned; and Joshua became their leader. Then God gave the order for his people to cross the River Jordan and begin the conquest of Canaan.

The time was ripe. For years Egypt had drained away the wealth of Canaan. But now Egypt was weak. And although the fortress cities of Canaan looked formidable to the Israelites, Canaan was weak too. The land was divided amongst a number of petty, feuding kingdoms. The Israelites crossed the river – and right in their path lay the city of Jericho.

Modern Jericho still depends on its age-old springs, which make it a green oasis. The mound of ancient Jericho can be seen in the distance.

Pottery, bones and skulls in an ancient burial cave at Jericho; reconstructed at the Rockefeller Museum, Jerusalem.

Jericho

Jericho has as long a history as perha[ps] any city in the world. From earliest times its fresh-water spring made it a[n] oasis in the surrounding desert. 'The[city of palms', it was called – and all[kinds of tropical fruits still grow ther[e] in the steaming heat of the Jordan Valley, far below sea level.

Before 6,000 BC there was a town on the site, with a stone wall, at least one tower, and a number of round houses. The fortified cities of Bible times were small by modern standards, though Jericho may have had several thousand citizens. But in times of war they became fortresses into which the people of the area could withdraw and be safe.

Long before Joshua's day Jericho was a strong fortress. It had two massive walls right round it – the outer one 6ft thick and 25-30ft high; the inner one 12ft thick. Splendid pottery, tables, stools, beds, baskets and daggers have been discovered in tombs dating from the time of Abraham, Isaac and Jacob.

No one knows what the city was like when Joshua first saw it. After the destruction and fire the site was abandoned for 400 years – and sun, wind and rain have left little trace of it. But we can be sure that Jericho was a daunting city for the nation's first test, after years in the open country. Israel would never have conquered it without God's help.

The Israelites blew their trumpets, as God commanded – and the walls of Jericho fell. From geography we know that Jericho lies in an earthquake zone. It may be that God used this 'natural' force to shake the city. After all, he is the Maker of our world. But

An ancient tower, part of the fortifications of old Jericho now being uncovered by archaeologists.

whatever it was, the Bible makes it clear that it was God who gave Jericho into his people's hands – fulfilling his promise made long, long before to give Abraham and his descendants a land of their own.

The ark of the covenant may have looked something like this drawing. It was an acacia wood chest with carrying poles overlaid with gold. And on top, overshadowing the 'mercy seat' with outspread wings, were two cherubim of hammered gold. Inside the ark were the commandments God had given his people. God designed the ark and the Israelites made it in the desert. It was the symbol of God's presence with them, and stood in the holiest place of all in the Tabernacle when the people set up camp.

Crossing the River Jordan

Rivers were a serious barrier to travellers in ancient times. In the dry summer season the River Jordan is only 30ft wide at Jericho and easy enough to ford. But the melting snows of early spring make it a raging torrent, overflowing both its banks. It was like this when God gave Joshua the order to take his people across. It seemed impossible. But higher up, at Adam, the river was dammed, holding the water back and allowing the Israelites to cross. The river banks have collapsed at this very spot several times since then – blocking the river. In our own century an earthquake caused a blockage lasting several hours.

In the story, God once again shows his perfect control over nature. Not until the priests carrying the ark had their feet actually in the water did it begin to go down.

Rahab

It is plain in the story that Rahab was not a good woman. But she was quick to realize that Jericho was helpless against the God of Israel. So she saved the lives of the two spies, and threw in her lot with the people of Israel. And God honoured her faith in him. She married an Israelite – and King David, and later Jesus himself, were descended from her.

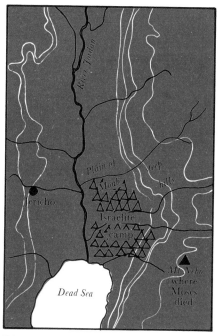

Places mentioned in the story

The Israelite camp was in the valley east of the River Jordan, facing Jericho. There were steep hills behind them, and the salt waters of the Dead Sea to the south. In the steamy tropical heat, Jericho – guarding the river crossing and the route into the hills – looked enticingly green and fertile.

A 'shofar' or ram's horn, the trumpet of ancient Israel. It was used to announce religious festivals, and also to call the people to war.

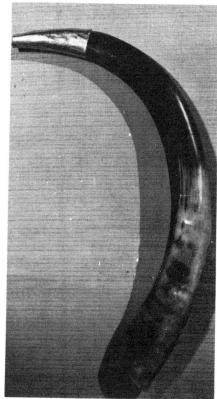

Mission Accomplished

The story of Samson

They had the place surrounded. The city gates had been bolted and barred. All other possible exits had been sealed off. Arms had been issued to every member of the force. And, to complete the security, the Special Squad had been called in to co-ordinate the operation.

People had been warned to keep off the streets. This man was extremely dangerous and there was likely to be violence. The police would not be held responsible for anybody who got in the way. When he'd been trapped before he'd reacted like a cornered rat. He'd lashed out and clubbed to death a thousand men before escaping.

'When you're dealing with that sort of madman,' the Chief of Police had been heard to say, 'you don't take chances. You go in with swords drawn – and ask questions later.'

But the big question of the moment was this: was he in the city at all? The truth was that they didn't really know. All they had to go on was an anonymous tip-off. But even the slightest chance that he was in the area was enough to alert the security forces and make them throw a cordon round the place.

Enemy sighted

According to their informer, he had entered the city under cover of darkness and had later been sighted in the quarter where the prostitutes traded. In all probability that was where he was now – but the Special Squad had advised against a raid. That would mean concentrating the entire force in one manoeuvre. In the event of the information being wrong – if he proved to be in some other corner of the city – word of the raid would spread like the plague . . . and Samson would get clean away.

No, the best plan was to just sit it out. If he *was* in Gaza, he would have to leave sooner or later – and that's when he would walk into the trap. If by morning there was still no sign of him, *then* – with daylight on their side – they would move in.

Meanwhile, all they could do was to wait . . . and it was the waiting they dreaded most. They hated being alone in the night with only stray dogs and their thoughts to haunt them. They could lash out at the dogs, of course – but nothing would drive away their thoughts. And each man's thoughts were the same: if Samson *was* here, would they be able to stop him – or would they, before morning, be so many corpses scattered along his escape route like houses lying smashed in the wake of a tornado?

The chances were that they would end up in som gutter or alleyway with their necks broken. For e perience had taught them that no body of men, n even the city police force, was match for this Samson this seemingly indestructible strong-man.

Muscle-power

That was the key – his strength. He wasn't real clever or shrewd; he couldn't outwit them. But the he didn't need to. It was his muscle-power – tha gargantuan force with which he had slain oth Philistines – which they could not seem to combat.

If only they could learn the secret of his strength discover the source of his incredible energy – the they might, just might, be able to nail him.

But optimism was hard to come by that night. Th pictures which flitted through the minds of Gaza policemen were not ones of victory, but of defeat . . well-worn memories of how Samson had previousl demonstrated his unearthly power. Unearthly it was and that, if only the Philistines had realized it, was

clue to the secret . . . for Samson was God's man; and his might was God's might!

Chosen by God

Even before his birth, Samson had been chosen by God to be a warrior – a powerful leader who would help his people, the Israelites, fight against the oppressive rule of the Philistines. Not that it was God's fault that his people were in such a spot. They had brought calamity upon themselves. God had given the land of Canaan to the Israelites, but they had failed to obey his command to drive out all the enemies around them. Instead they settled for the easier course of living side by side with these other races and their pagan beliefs. In order to improve relationships they began to intermarry . . . and this led to the adoption of the foreigners' cultures – and the worship of their heathen gods.

More than once the Israelites had forsaken the living God – the God who had delivered them from slavery in Egypt and established them in a land of their own. And this was the most terrible – and hurtful – insult to him.

God had a purpose for the Israelites. They were to show the world that there is only one true God. And each time they forgot this and took up the empty religions of their neighbours, God stepped in with a punishment which pulled them up with a start and turned them back to himself. Ironically, the price they often had to pay was subjection to the very nations they had tried to befriend.

Threat to the Philistines

Each time the Israelites cried to him for help, God would select and appoint a leader to free them from their oppressors. Samson was just such a leader. But *what* a leader! Dedicated to God from birth, and endowed with special strength, this man could rip apart the jaws of a lion as though it were some feeble young goat! In a fit of temper, he had once caught three hundred jackals with his own bare hands, tied their tails together in pairs, with a flaming torch between each pair, and set them loose in the Philistines' cornfields, burning the crops to the ground.

That was a sight the Philistines wouldn't forget in a hurry. And as the policemen of Gaza crouched in the shadows, waiting to pounce on their prey, it was a picture which more than once came to mind. It was, after all, the incident which really established Samson as a threat to Philistine rule. They saw it as a deliberate act of defiance, challenging their authority. And that was exactly what it was, for it was all part of God's plan to trap the Philistines and break their hold over the Israelites.

The Philistines took up the challenge immediately, retaliating by taking Samson's wife and father-in-law and burning them alive (for it was because his Philistine father-in-law had given Samson's wife to another man that he had burned down the crops).

When Samson learned what had happened, he hunted out the men who had murdered his wife and viciously battered them to death.

Raiding party

Incensed, the Philistines sent a raiding party to Lehi, in Judah, where Samson was thought to be living, to track him down and kill him. Mercilessly, they turned the town upside down – but the strongman was nowhere to be seen.

Fearing for their own lives, the men of Judah agreed to deliver Samson to the Philistines. But they weren't too sure that their leader would come quietly. There would certainly be some grisly scenes if he turned on them. So they sent a force of three thousand men to bring him in.

But Samson wasn't going to harm his own people – God had called him to deliver them, not to increase their suffering. So, having extracted from them a promise that they themselves would not kill him, he allowed them to bind him with strong, new ropes and lead him back to Lehi.

The strength of the Lord

When Samson saw the Philistines, his God-given strength surged through him! He snapped the ropes as easily as woollen thread, picked up a donkey's jawbone that was lying on the ground, and laid into his enemies, lashing out and sending them flying.

By the time he had finished, one thousand men lay dead! Who could blame the policemen of Gaza for quaking in their boots at the thought that they too might be despatched from this world just as swiftly and brutally – and at any minute!

But as it happened, they had a few hours to wait – a few more hours to spend chewing their nails as they pondered their chances of survival. For it was after midnight before Samson appeared.

He came at them suddenly, like a spectre out of the night, bearing down upon them, ready to do battle.

But where was the man who would be first to thrust his sword at the strong-man's throat? Who would be first to spend his life for the Philistine cause? Who would gladly be the night's first martyr?

'Attack!' came the command. But not one man stirred.

'Attack!' But the boots of the Gaza police force were inexplicably filled with lead.

This was ridiculous! These were trained men – a fighting force drilled to jump to every order! But not tonight. Courage, if there had been any, had fled . . . The cohesion with which they had so often responded and fought forsook them . . . In the place of valiant officers of the law stood shivering wrecks . . . The whole operation had become a shambles! A farce!

Messenger of death

Samson strode nearer, his threatening form silhouetted against the yellow glow of their torches. Suddenly he seemed ten feet tall! A massive messenger of death from the very bowels of hell!

'Run for it!' Every man had thought it, but not till one screamed the words did they dare to move. Then it was every man for himself. Run! Get away! Hide!

There would be a price to pay for this. Cowardice carried a harsh sentence. But even the commander of the Special Squad could not help but tremble as he watched, incredulous, as the enemy made his escape.

It was just not possible – but it was happening! Samson was *lifting* the city gates, wrenching the posts clean out of the ground! Would he toss them aside as so much matchwood and sprint off into the darkness? No! He would show these Philistines what he was made of! He would teach these heathen dogs to fear the power of the living God!

With one uncanny move he swept the city gates up on to his shoulders . . . and was gone!

The secret of his strength

It took the Philistines some time to recover from that blow. For although he had not so much as laid a finger on one man that night, Samson had assaulted their minds with the most unnerving display of strength they had ever been unfortunate enough to witness.

When finally they could discuss the matter unemotionally, they were all agreed on one thing. They *must* learn the secret of his strength. Only then would they ever be able to defeat him. But how?

The answer came one day, quite by chance, when word reached the Philistines that Samson had fallen in love with a girl named Delilah, who lived over in the Valley of Sorek. Perhaps his weakness for this girl could be made his undoing . . . So the head men of the five Philistine cities went personally to visit Delilah.

'There's a lot of money in this for you,' they said, 'provided you do as we say. Eleven hundred pieces of silver from each of us – and all you have to do is get him to tell you what makes him so strong. Shouldn't be difficult for a girl like you . . .'

Nobody's fool

So the trap was set. The next time Samson came to visit the girl, she asked him outright what was the secret of his strength.

But Samson was nobody's fool. He told her: 'If I were tied with seven raw leather bowstrings, I'd be no stronger than the next man.'

Delilah passed this on to the Philistine leaders and they arranged for her to be given the bowstrings. When Samson fell asleep on the girl's lap, she was to tie him up and then call out: 'Samson! The Philistines are here!' If Samson couldn't break out of the bonds,

the Philistines, who would be hiding in the next room, would rush in and seize him.

But when Delilah called, Samson awoke and snapped the thongs as though they had been wool!

'You lied to me,' cried the girl, 'and made fun of me! Now tell me the truth – what makes you so strong?'

Samson was amused. It was a harmless little game. 'If you were to tie me with new ropes,' he told her, 'I'd be helpless.'

Again Delilah lulled Samson to sleep – and again he awoke and broke out of the ropes.

Delilah was furious. She wasn't going to let a fortune slip through her fingers that easily. Again she asked for the secret.

Samson was enjoying the game – but he was also beginning to weaken.

'If you were to weave my hair into your loom . . .' he teased.

So, while he slept, the girl wove . . . but when Samson awoke he jumped up and tore his hair from the loom, breaking it.

His enemies crept in . . .

The Philistines thought it would never work. But the girl nagged and nagged Samson day after day until at last, fed up to the teeth with her pestering, he bawled: 'Oh, for goodness' sake, woman! If you really *must* know, my strength lies in my hair! It's not been cut from the day I was born, and must *never* be cut – God commanded it! If anyone were to take a razor to it, my strength would leave me.'

Needless to say, Delilah informed the Philistines – and the next time Samson slept on the girl's lap, his enemies crept in and cut off his hair.

'Samson! The Philistines are here!' called Delilah.

Samson awoke and thought, 'I'll jump up and break free, just as I did before!' But this time it was different. Samson had broken the Nazarite vow made before he was born. He had shown how little his dedication to God meant to him. And God had left him. His strength had disappeared – and his enemies pounced.

Clapped in irons

Immediately they gouged out his eyes so that, if by some miracle he were suddenly to regain his strength,

he would not be able to see his captors and strike out at them.

Pain raced through his body, blurring all his thoughts and senses . . . and the next thing he knew he was being clapped in irons in a smelly dungeon in Gaza. There he was set to work – humiliating, women's work – grinding at the prison mill like some dumb beast.

News of the arrest came to the people of Gaza like the 'all clear' after an epidemic. There was dancing in the streets, wild drinking parties, and hysterical

religious ceremonies as the people praised and sacrificed to their god Dagon.

'We shall hold a great festival in the temple,' planned the Philistine leaders. 'Our god has given Samson into our hands.' So the preparations were made. And on the day three thousand people crammed the building to overflowing. Drinks were 'on the house' and within a short time the people were falling over one another, blind drunk.

'Bring out that murderer so we can make fun of him and torment him!' came the cry – and the officials were only too pleased to oblige. This would be the crowning point of their great victory! The once mighty Samson, arch-enemy of the Philistines, humiliated and abused!

But Samson had done some hard thinking in prison. His pride and his strength had gone, but he was still God's man. His capture had brought dishonour to God; but now, through him, God would have the last word. For no one had really noticed – but Samson's hair had begun to grow again . . .

Then Samson prayed . . .

As the prisoner was led out into the centre of the temple to stand between the two pillars which supported the roof, the jeers crescendoed to fever pitch. Rotten fruit was thrown; abuse was hurled.

Samson called to the lad who had led him from the dungeon. 'Here, boy – place my hands on the two pillars; I want to rest against them.'

The youth did as he was requested . . . then Samson prayed. 'O Lord God, remember me! Give me back my strength just one more time, so that I can get my own back on these Philistines for the loss of at least one of my eyes . . .'

And God heard! And Samson pushed!

Fraction by fraction, inch by inch, the pillars began to shift . . .

'Let me die with the Philistines!' Samson cried. But his prayer was lost in a deafening 'crack!' as the pillars shifted and gave way – bringing the ceiling, then the walls, crashing down around the Philistines, engulfing everyone in the building.

A blow for God

Samson, truly the strongest man in the world, had a remarkable epitaph: 'He slew more enemies of Israel at the time of his death than he slew during his entire lifetime.'

He would have been proud of that. Not because he was a cold-blooded murderer who revelled in the death of his foes. But because he had struck a major blow for his God. He had begun the deliverance of his people. And that, after all, was the very task for which he had been born.

Mission accomplished.

Samson/**Fact-finder**

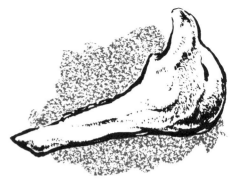

Bible passage
You will find this story in Judges 14 –
16. Judges 13 tells the story of
Samson's birth. Hebrews 11:32, in the
New Testament, includes Samson in a
list of the great heroes of God who
'through faith fought whole countries
and won . . . They were weak but
became strong; they were mighty in
battle and defeated the armies of
foreigners.'

Time
About 1070 BC.

Setting of the story in history
This story, like the story of Gideon
(told in *Great Adventures of the Bible*)
belongs to the time of the Judges,
perhaps 200 years after the people of
Israel left Egypt, and 160 years after
the fall of Jericho (the previous story
in this book).

While Joshua was alive he held the
nation together. He held them to
God's purpose of making the land of
Canaan their own. They succeeded in
driving out the enemy nations, north
and south. Canaan was divided up
amongst the 12 tribes of Israel and the
people settled down to make homes for
themselves and cultivate the land.

But they had not driven all the
foreigners out. And when they were
scattered, and no longer had a strong
national leader, they gradually began
to adopt pagan ways – and pagan gods.
As one people, united in obedience to
God, they had been strong. Now there
was nothing to hold them together.
They were weak – and an easy prey
once more to the enemy nations
around.

The Canaanites in the north
attacked and recovered their lost land.
The people of Moab moved in from
the south-east; the Midianites crossed
the River Jordan from the east; the
Philistines moved in from the south-
west . . . Israel suffered under one
oppressing nation after another. Yet
each time God's people called to him
for help, he sent a leader to deliver
them (these are the 12 'Judges' of the
book of Judges). But as soon as they
were free, they forgot God again.

For 40 years the Israelites in the
south were subject to the Philistines.
Then God sent Samson.

The Philistines
About 100 years before Samson was
born, powerful Egypt was on full alert
Invasion was imminent. They had
received a succession of terrifying
reports: foreign ships were sailing
down the coast; overland an unknown
people were trekking south – men,
women, children, waggons and carts
and before them went an army.
Everywhere they went they burnt
houses, destroyed cities, and ruined
crops. The great Hittite Empire
(present-day Turkey) fell before them

These were the 'Sea Peoples', and
amongst them were the Philistines.
The Egyptians defeated them in a
great naval battle, and drove the army
back from the border. But very soon
afterwards the Philistines were firmly
settled in strong cities on the coastal
plain of Canaan: Ashkelon, Ashdod,
Ekron, Gaza and Gath. They were
there when the Israelite invasion
began. And as the Israelites weakened

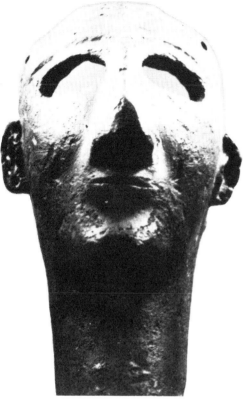

*Head of Baal, whom the Canaanites
worshipped as god of weather and of
fertility.*

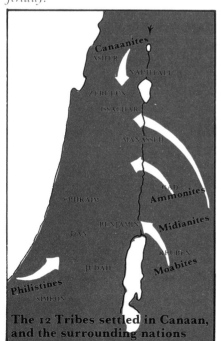

**The 12 Tribes settled in Canaan,
and the surrounding nations**

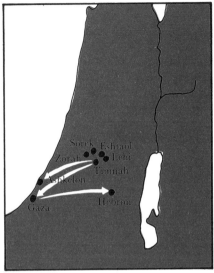

The soldiers of Pharaoh Ramesses III plunder the ox-carts of the invading Philistines. After their defeat the Philistines turned back to settle in Canaan.

they moved in up the long valleys from the coast to control the Israelite hill-country.

The Philistines brought with them their own style of dress; beautiful, decorated pottery of Greek design;

and – most important of all – from the land of the Hittites, the secret of how to smelt iron.

The Philistines guarded their secret well. They traded in iron, but kept their monopoly. So the Israelites, too poor to buy what they needed, were without iron weapons and without farm tools of iron. And iron was a much tougher, more practical metal than bronze. The Israelites were confined to the hills because the people on the plain had chariots reinforced with iron.

Samson's vow

From before he was born, Samson was under the Nazarite vow of dedication to God. He was set apart for a special purpose. As an outward sign of this he was pledged never to take wine (people's normal drink in Canaan at that time) or any strong drink; to keep strictly to the Israelite food-laws; and never to cut his hair. When Samson allowed Delilah to cut his hair, he broke his vow – and God withdrew the special power he had been given.

It is clear from the story that Samson was often wilful and wrong-headed. He abused the special power God gave him to deliver Israel from the Philistines – and in the end he suffered terribly for his disobedience. His capture brought dishonour on God's name: allowing the Philistines to think that their idol Dagon was greater than the living God. The Bible never hides or glosses over the weaknesses and sins of its heroes. We are not meant to imitate Samson's actions. But he does set us an example of faith. God can – and does – make something of even the worst of us, if we let him.

How could God tolerate – and even command – the killing and destruction described in the book of Judges? This is a hard question. We know that God loves and wants the best for each one of us. But he is also a just God, and if men and women go on refusing to listen to him, and persecuting his people, there comes a time when God acts in judgement. He cannot allow wrong to go unpunished for ever. This applied to Israel's enemies. It also applies to God's own people, when they persist in wrongdoing.

Places mentioned in the story

Samson was born at Zorah, on the north side of the broad valley of Sorek (Delilah's home), which runs up from the Mediterranean plain to within 13 miles of Jerusalem. He married his Philistine wife at Timnah, 4 miles away across the valley. He attacked the Philistines in their own strongholds at Ashkelon, on the coast, and at nearby Gaza, where he died.

Remains of Ashkelon – scene of Samson's exploits – dating mainly from Roman times.

A Philistine warship.

Giant-killer Hits the Headlines

The story of David and Goliath

Let's get one thing straight: a reporter's life is not the cushy number it's made out to be, not by a long chalk. All right, so there are the occasional perks, and some jobs – like covering the king's garden parties or writing up the ladies' fashion shows – are a piece of cake. You usually get a buffet lunch thrown in, so you can't really complain they're boring. And I've got to be honest, the pay's not bad and I do get a donkey allowance.

On the other hand, you have to work all sorts of hours – especially when you're with a small newspaper like the *Bethlehem Star*. And you're expected to be out in all weathers. If a story breaks on a bitterly cold night, when the rest of Canaan is sensibly tucked up in bed, *you* have to brave the wintry blast and sniff out the news. And, believe me, you have to dig! Scoops don't just fall into your lap like so much manna from heaven!

Not that I was ever afraid of a bit of hard work. What does bug me, though, is this thing about holidays. You can have your leave – a full two weeks – any time you like, *providing* no big story comes up. If that happens, and it's up to the Chief Scribe to decide what constitutes a 'big story', you can forget about your leave until a 'more convenient time'.

Battle zone

Now you're probably wondering what all this has to do with David. Well, let me tell you that I've got *him* to thank for one such ruined holiday! Our bags were packed. The wife had had her hair done, the kids had been scrubbed, and we were all ready to set off for a fortnight with the wife's family, down at Beersheba. I was just loading up the donkey when the messenger boy from the office came steaming into the yard as though his tail was on fire! His untimely arrival could mean only one thing: the holiday was off.

The reason, it turned out, was that the Chief, who claims he can sense when a story is about to break – and he can – wanted me to join my fellow newshound at the 'battle zone'. At that time the Israelite and Philistine armies were perched on opposite sides of a valley about 15 miles from Bethlehem, slinging little more than abuse at each other. But the Chief had been up there testing the military temperature and he'd come away with the definite impression that it was near boiling-point.

When the pot boiled over, he said, he wanted full coverage of the story – and one man couldn't produce that . . . which is how I came to be standing with the Israelite army, looking across Elah Valley into the jaws of the Philistines. And I hadn't been there long before those 'jaws' opened, as you might say, and out stepped Goliath – a towering giant whose very appearance was sufficient to stun the Israelite troops into silence.

Nightmare

Goliath was a formidable sight. A walking nightmare – dressed up in flesh and blood and striding in our direction! Standing about ten feet tall, he was almost totally encased in armour – bronze helmet, mail-coat (that alone must have weighed around nine stone) and bronze leggings. Ahead of him came his armour-bearer, carrying (or rather, struggling with) his shield. I wouldn't have liked to guess its weight, but I'd take a bet that two Israelite soldiers could have stood behind it, side by side, and nobody would have known they were there! Slung at the giant's side was a huge sword – a two-handed affair for any average-sized man – and in his hand was an enormous spear. It had a shaft several inches thick, and a vicious iron head which must have weighed a stone at least. Not the sort of man you'd go out of your way to upset, as you can imagine! But on that morning he didn't need upsetting. He was in a fighting mood already.

Challenge

A little way from the Philistine front line he stopped, raised his spear threateningly, and boomed out his challenge across the valley.

'Why spill the blood of a whole army?' he roared. 'This can be settled in single combat! I'll fight for the Philistines – you choose your own champion. If your man is lucky enough to kill me, then the Philistines will be your servants; but if I am the victor, you Israelites will be our slaves. I defy the armies of Israel! If you dare, send out a man to make war with me!' (That was the gist of it, anyway. I don't remember the exact words.)

Reason to be scared

The effect of the challenge in the Israelite camp was pretty unnerving for a civilian. All of a sudden I no longer felt safe. I saw great Israelite warriors literally shaking with fright, and almost beginning to panic. I remember looking round to note King Saul's reaction. He seemed as disturbed as everyone else.

Now you might think that they had every reason to be scared, and maybe, on the face of it, they had. No man, not even Israel's king, who was the

tallest of the Israelites, fancied his chances against this Philistine monster. But as an army – a full fighting force – what did they have to be afraid of? Only a small number of the enemy force were giants like Goliath. They came from Gath, which isn't far from the valley. And according to a copy of the old *Lachish Echo* that I used for reference when I wrote up my story, the Israelites attacked and defeated all the giants of Gath when fighting under Joshua.

Admittedly that was a couple of hundred years ago, but the men who faced Goliath were descendants of those fearless troops. On top of that, they weren't without a great leader. Saul, our first king, had proved himself a bold and shrewd commander in previous times of war. Most important of all, our God was the same God who had fought for Joshua ... so why, I wondered, were the troops afraid of the Philistines now?

Elementary lesson

Looking back, I think maybe it had something to do with the change in King Saul. God appointed him king only because the people demanded it. And Saul disobeyed God's clear command in the battle against the Amalekites. So God rejected him. Saul knew this meant that victory was no longer guaranteed, so he wasn't going to fight unless it became absolutely necessary.

Apart from that, I reckon that God was using the occasion to introduce young David – whom he had already singled out to succeed Saul as king – to the Israelite people ... And he intended to remind them, through David, that victory depends not on human strength but on trust and obedience to God's leading.

It was a rather elementary lesson, I know, but it was taught in such a remarkable way that no one is ever likely to forget it.

Imagine: there was the Israelite army, desperately racking its brains to find a solution to Goliath's challenge – feverishly seeking deliverance by means of

some military device or tactical manoeuvre – when along came God's answer . . . a peasant shepherd boy, with no more than a staff and a sling to fight with, and not so much as a day's army training under his belt.

Of course, the fact that he was a Bethlehem lad made it all the more interesting from the newspaper's point of view – a sort of 'local boy makes good' story.

Reward

I first came across this lad when I was doing an interview piece with one of the officers. David had been sent to the battlefront by his father to deliver some extra rations to his three eldest brothers, who had volunteered for this campaign, and to check that they were fit and well. While he was talking with them, Goliath stepped from the Philistine ranks to deliver his challenge yet again (for the eightieth time!). The Israelites, who had taken up their battle stations, turned and raced back to the camp site. In the panic I lost sight of the lad, but I soon found him again. This time he was talking to some other soldiers. They were explaining that King Saul had offered a reward to anyone who could kill the giant.

'What sort of reward?' David asked.

I wondered whether this could be the story I had been sent to cover, and moved closer.

'For a start,' explained the soldiers, 'Goliath's killer will receive a lot of money. On top of that, his family will no longer have to pay taxes – and he'll be able to marry one of the king's daughters.'

But David didn't seem particularly interested in any reward – at least, not for himself.

'Who does this heathen Philistine think he is!' he said angrily. 'How dare he defy the army of the living God!'

The big story

I knew I was on to something then. I sensed that, impossible though it might seem, if anybody was willing to accept Goliath's challenge, it would be this lad.

But just then Eliab, David's eldest brother, came by – and it looked for a moment as if that would be the end of it. 'You still here?' he snapped at David. 'You're supposed to be on your way home – you've got sheep to look after, remember! Don't hang about here, skiving, you cocky little brat! I know you only came to watch the battle. Now push off!'

'What have I done wrong now?' said David. 'I only asked a question!'

And he carried on asking the same question . . . until the question reached the ears of the king – and David was sent for. This was it. This was going to be the big story.

Ridiculous suggestion

David was led to the king's tent, and I strung along behind, positioning myself within ear-shot. But I couldn't believe what I heard!

'You've got nothing to worry about,' said David. 'Leave this Philistine to me.'

Saul was amused. The boy was plucky, he'd give

him that. Not that it made any difference. The suggestion was ridiculous. 'That monster would make mincemeat of you!' Saul said.

But David meant business. 'When I'm looking after my father's sheep,' he told the king, 'and a lion or bear comes and snatches away a lamb, I go after it with a club and rescue the lamb from its mouth. And if the beast turns on me, I grab it by the jaws and beat it to death. I'll do the same to this bragging Philistine! I'll teach him to humiliate the army of the living God! And the Lord God who has saved me from the lion and bear will save me from this heathen beast!'

Saul didn't like the idea, but eventually he consented. 'Very well – go ahead. And God go with you!'

Five smooth stones

Saul had David dressed up in his own armour, and we watched as he was strapped in. Believe me, it was a comical sight! Everything was too big, and David complained that it was too heavy – so he took it off. Then he went to a nearby stream, chose five smooth stones, slipped them into his shepherd's bag, and went off down into the valley.

Now it was Goliath's turn to be insulted. As he strode down towards David, he roared out: 'What! You come at me with a stick? Am I a dog? Come over here and I'll throw your body to the birds and wild animals!'

The Israelite soldiers looked on, flabbergasted – and

shuddered. He staggered back for a moment – then he fell forward and thudded to the ground.

The two armies held their breath. Was the Philistine only stunned or . . . ?

The young shepherd boy left them in no doubt; if he wasn't dead, he soon would be. Reaching the sprawled form, David drew the huge sword from its sheath – and cut off the giant's head.

Scene of defeat

Immediately there was uproar in the Philistine camp! Their champion was dead – the battle lost! Panic and fear gripped every heart, and the enemy scrambled over tents, equipment, and even one another, just to get away from that scene of defeat.

Needless to say, the Israelites were hard on their heels. And they fought and killed the Philistine soldiers all along the roads to their heathen cities.

So that was it. The Lord had his victory; David slew his Goliath; the Israelites retained their freedom – and the *Bethlehem Star* got its story.

But, as I said, *I* didn't get my holiday. I don't blame David, of course; in fact, I've a lot to thank him for. In the years since then he's provided the material for numerous front page stories. I'd stop and tell you about some of them if I had the time – but the messenger boy's just arrived. Apparently a big story has just broken over in Jerusalem.

It would have to happen on a night like this . . .

quite embarrassed by the lad's courage. But it was his faith which really staggered them.

David yelled: 'You come to me with a sword and spear and shield – but I come to you in the name of the Lord . . . the Lord God of the armies of heaven and of Israel, whom you dare to defy. Today God will destroy you! I will kill you and cut off your head! And the bodies of the Philistines will become food for the birds, so that the whole world will know that the God of Israel is the only God. And all these Israelite troops will know that God doesn't need man's weapons to save his people – for this is his battle . . . and he has already given you to us!'

Missile

Without wasting another word, Goliath stormed down towards his opponent – and David ran to meet him! Taking a stone from his bag, he slipped it into his sling, whirled it over his head – and let the missile fly . . . straight to its mark! Without a sound, it crashed into the giant's forehead – the only part of his massive frame that was unprotected. His whole body

David/**Fact-finder**

Bible passage
You will find this story in 1 Samuel 17.
1 Samuel 16 tells how Samuel anointed
David as God's chosen king. The rest
of 1 Samuel and 2 Samuel contain the
story of David's life. His death is
described in 1 Kings 1.

Time
About 1020 BC.

Setting of the story in history
This story takes us into a new period
of Israel's history. The rule of the
Judges is over. Samson, the last of
these great champions has been dead
perhaps 50 years. Now there is a king
on the throne – Israel's first king, Saul.

The Judges were all very well, but
the people of Israel clamoured for a
king to lead them, like the other
nations. The prophet Samuel was
upset about this. To his mind the
people were rejecting God as their
leader. He warned them that kings
brought trouble – the burden of taxes
and forced labour and compulsory
call-up to the army. But the people
were insistent, and God allowed them
to have their way.

Saul was anointed king. He was
young and strong and tall and
handsome. The people were pleased
with their king. The nation found a
new unity under his leadership. But
King Saul began to get above himself.
He thought he knew better than the
old prophet Samuel. He went his own
way, and disobeyed God. And God in
turn rejected Saul. The next king
would be a man 'after God's own
heart'.

That man was still only a boy,
shepherding his father's sheep in the
hills round Bethlehem – the youngest
of eight brothers. But God was already
training David for greatness. He had
learnt how to deal with marauding
lions and bears. Then came the great
test – single combat with the giant
Goliath. David for Israel – Goliath for
the Philistines.

*A shepherd-boy using his sling, as David
would have done. He had to keep constant
watch over his flock to protect it from
marauding wild animals.*

Left: *The sling was used in warfare from
early times. Two slingers of the Assyrian
army.*

Right: *A Philistine soldier amongst
captives taken by Ramesses III. He wears
the warrior's tassled kilt and plumed
helmet.*

Places mentioned in the story

The two armies faced one another across the Valley of Elah – Israelites on the north side; Philistines on the south. David's father sent him west over the hills from Bethlehem with food for his soldier-brothers. When their champion was killed, the Philistines fled west to Gath and Ekron, their strongholds on the plain.

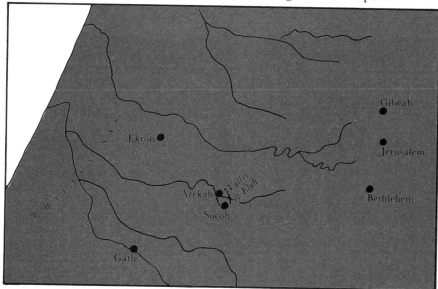

The Philistines

You can read how the Philistines came to Canaan on the Samson Fact-finder pages. Samson did not check the Philistines for long. They were soon pushing inland again up the valleys from the coastal plain to the Israelite territory on the hills. Goliath's death was a set-back – but the Philistines were not finished. In a new battle on Mount Gilboa in the north, the Philistines killed King Saul. And in the years that followed, David fought many bitter campaigns against them before he succeeded in establishing his border.

David and Goliath

The fully-armed Goliath shows what formidable opponents the Philistines could be. Quite apart from his extraordinary height (over 10ft), he was almost totally encased in armour – protected by a helmet; coat of mail; greaves on his legs; and a huge shield. He was armed with sword and spear. The spear-head was made of iron, the new wonder-metal of which the Philistines had a virtual monopoly. The rest was of the traditional bronze.

The king of Israel had his own armour, it's true – but David carried nothing but his shepherd's sling. The sling offered no protection – but it was a powerful offensive weapon, all the same. There were slingers in the armies of Egypt (and later Assyria and Babylonia) as well as in the Israelite army. The sling was made of leather, broader in the middle, to hold the stone. Holding both ends the slinger would whirl the sling round his head, suddenly letting go one end to hurl the stone at colossal speed. David had had plenty of practice. He did not miss. The giant didn't stand a chance!

helmet

spear with iron tip

shield

mail coat

sword

stones

greaves

sling

God's Thunderbolt
The story of Elijah

The password was 'lamb's blood'. That was only for a week, of course. It had to be changed every Sabbath. Otherwise King Ahab's spies might gain access to one of the meetings and report back that there were still some of his subjects who were worshipping the God of Israel. The penalty for attending such a service could be death. For God, according to Queen Jezebel, was *not* God of Israel, and any 'heretic' caught worshipping him or singing his praises would pay in blood.

It was the ultimate irony in Israel's history. The God who had nurtured them from the seed of one man into a vast nation was an outcast in his own land. The Lord who had delivered them from slavery in Egypt was a 'strange god'. The Father who had led them into this beautiful land and given them victory in their battles, a settled, prosperous life and all home comforts was now the subject of mockery and humiliation.

Lifeless idols

Ahab had played his part in this. From the first day of his reign he had encouraged the people of Israel to bow down to the lifeless idols in their heathen shrines. As if that wasn't bad enough, he married Jezebel, a foreign princess who worshipped Baal, the fertility god of the Canaanites. Then they built a temple and altar to Baal and led the nation into idol worship.

But Jezebel was evil personified. She wasn't content with inviting the Israelites to follow Baal. She set about exterminating every last trace of the old religion. The prophets of God were to be hunted down and killed – and any persons found worshipping God must be 'persuaded' to denounce him and follow Baal.

Which was why God's faithful people – only a few thousand out of the entire population – had to meet in secret. It was like an 'underground church' formed at a time of religious persecution. Never before had the followers of the living God had to resort to using a password.

A champion for God

As they met together in the dank gloom of the foot-hill caves, they cried once more to God to step in and rescue them from this spiritual bondage; to stamp out the blasphemous worship of Baal; and to deal with Ahab and his corrupt queen.

Yet, as they prayed, they couldn't help but wonder whether God would ever answer them. It had been years since he had last raised up a deliverer for Israel. Why, the country hadn't seen a leader who truly followed God since King David. How they longed for another David – another champion of Israel.

But what was needed wasn't a champion for Israel – it was a champion for God.

He was on his way . . .

Judgement

His name was Elijah. But if he'd had a nickname it would have been 'God's thunderbolt' – for he exploded into Israel's history with all the suddenness and impact of an electrical charge from the heavens. When he

spoke, his words were a torrent of fire. And when he prayed, God's fury was unleashed in judgement.

That judgement was to fall on the shoulders of King Ahab – for he had done more to provoke God to anger than any of the kings before him. And the repercussions would be felt throughout the land. It began the day Elijah confronted King Ahab and told him: 'As surely as the Lord God of Israel lives – the God whose servant I am and by whose authority I speak – Israel will see no more rain nor dew for years to come . . . until *I* give the word.'

The king didn't need the minister of agriculture to interpret such an announcement. The meaning was clear: disaster! Drought was no stranger in Israel.

e people and livestock alike had adjusted to being
thout water from time to time. But no rain at all –
t even a single drop of morning dew – for years?
was unthinkable! It was as good as passing the
ath sentence on the entire nation . . . if the threat
s to be taken seriously. After all, Baal was god

full-scale manhunt to find the only person who could
command the skies to open and bring down the rain.

But though they searched the land from end to end,
the prophet Elijah was nowhere to be found.

'This is impossible!' stormed the king. 'A man cannot just vanish! He must be hiding – and if he's
hiding, he can be found!'

Which was true. But Elijah wasn't simply hiding
himself. He was being hidden – by God.

Amazing news

After he had delivered his message to Ahab, Elijah
had set up camp beside Cherith Brook, to the east
of where it flows into the River Jordan. On God's
command, the ravens had brought him meat and
bread each morning and evening, and the brook
provided all the water he could drink.

Eventually, though, the brook became a trickle and

the weather . . . wouldn't he look after his new
orshippers?

Iessages of doom

t first it was the source of much amusement in the
ng's court. Surely this Elijah was a laughable
gure – a madman who derived some sort of morbid
leasure from spreading messages of doom! But as the
n burnt down from a cloudless sky day after day,
en week after week, the smiles began to fade from
e corridors of the king's palace.

Moistureless weeks rolled into bone-dry months . . .
e crops failed . . . the animals died . . . the earth
ardened and cracked . . . and the king launched a

dried up. Then God told Elijah to go to the village
of Zarephath, on the coast near Sidon city. There he
would find a widow who would feed him, for God
had told her to expect the prophet.

When Elijah reached Zarephath, however, he found
the woman despondent. 'I've only a little cooking oil
and a handful of flour left in the house,' she said. 'I
was going to make one last meal for myself and my
son . . . and then we must starve.'

'Don't talk like that!' said Elijah. 'First bake me a
bread roll – and afterwards you'll still have enough
to feed yourself and your son.'

The woman was baffled; but there was more
amazing news yet to come!

'God says you'll *always* have plenty of oil and flour in the jars – right up to the time he sends rain for the crops to grow again.'

And God kept his word – for however much the woman poured out for each meal, the level of the oil and corn in the jars never went down!

Sworn statement

Something else which didn't go down during those three years was Ahab's blood pressure! Desperate to locate Elijah and to persuade him to pray for rain, the king had sent to the heads of all the neighbouring countries, demanding that they search their domains for Elijah. He even insisted that they sign a sworn statement to say that the prophet was not hiding within their boundaries.

Of course, Elijah was never found. God would not be rushed. He had elected a day on which his prophet would face Ahab again . . . and when that day arrived, the message came to Elijah very simply and clearly: 'I will soon send rain again. Go and tell King Ahab.'

Dedicated follower

So Elijah headed for Samaria, where the king's palace was. On the way he came across Obadiah, the head of the king's household affairs, who was out searching for grass for the king's horses.

Curiously, Obadiah was a dedicated follower of God. That being so, how he ever obtained such an important position, let alone kept it, is a mystery. You'd have thought Jezebel would have had him demoted, if not beheaded, long ago. But somehow he had escaped her efforts to wipe out all worship of the God of Israel. Either he was a 'secret' follower, like so many others in the land, or else he was so very good at his job that the king and queen overlooked his 'heretical' beliefs.

But there was one thing Jezebel would not have overlooked, had she found out. During one of her most heated purges, Obadiah had hidden a hundred of God's prophets in two caves – fifty in each – and had kept them fed with bread and water until the pressure eased up.

A braver, more faithful man it would have been hard to find. But when he heard Elijah's request that he should 'tell the king that I am here', he felt anything but bold.

'You're asking me to go to my death!' said Obadiah. 'Don't you know that the king has searched *everywhere* for you? If I go to tell him you're here, who knows if the Spirit of the Lord won't come and take you off somewhere else? If Ahab comes and you're not here, my head will roll!'

But Elijah told him: 'I promise you, as surely as the Lord lives, that I will face Ahab this day.'

Supernatural showdown

When Ahab arrived he roared at Elijah: 'So, it *is* you! You're the one who brought this disaster on Israel!'

'You are wrong,' said the prophet. 'You and your predecessors are to blame for this drought and famine, because you have forsaken God and worshipped Baal instead!'

Before the king had a chance to reply, Elijah went on: 'Call all the people of Israel to Mount Carmel and bring the four hundred and fifty prophets of Baal and the four hundred prophets of Asherah, the mother-goddess.'

So the king did as Elijah had said. And when all the people were assembled on the mountain, the prophet addressed them.

'How long will you hover between two opinions? the Lord is God, follow him! But if Baal is God, the follow him!'

Elijah waited for the people's reaction, but the were speechless. What could they say?

Then Elijah continued: 'Listen, I'm the onl prophet of the Lord left – but Baal has four hundre and fifty prophets! Let them, then, bring two bullock They can choose whichever one they like and cut it in pieces. Then they can put wood on their altar and la the bullock on the wood. But they mustn't *light* th wood.

'I'll do the same, placing the bullock on the woo on the Lord's altar – but I won't light the wood.

'Then the prophets of Baal will pray, calling on th name of their gods, and I will pray, calling on th name of the Lord. The God who answers by sendin fire to light the wood on his altar is God indeed!'

The people agreed, saying, 'Good idea! That's a ver fair test!'

And a test it was to be – a contest, in fact, of divin strength . . . a sort of supernatural showdown tha would prove beyond all doubt who was the *true* God the *only* God.

The tiniest spark

Elijah turned to the prophets of Baal. 'You go first he said. 'For there are many of you and you can hav the bullock ready in no time.'

So they did as Elijah had suggested, preparing th bullock and laying it on the wood on their altar. The they began praying, calling out: 'O Baal, hear us!'

But there was no fire. So they called and calle and called all morning. But there wasn't so much the tiniest spark.

Then they began dancing and leaping around th

altar, as though their cavorting would induce their god to speak with flames. But this didn't work either.

Elijah, who had held his tongue till now, couldn't hold out any longer and started mocking them.

'You'll have to do better than that!' he scoffed. 'Shout louder – perhaps your god is out nattering to somebody – or sitting on the loo! Or maybe he's gone off on his holidays – or fallen asleep! Come on, shout louder if you want to wake him up!'

The prophets of Baal were enraged; Elijah was making fools of them! How much longer would their god allow them to go on like this? Why wouldn't he send fire to shut up this big-mouthed prophet of the Lord? Perhaps if they presented their own blood to him he would be stirred into action!

So they took knives and swords and slashed at their arms until the blood gushed out! But there was still no sign of any fire. Blindly they carried on, ranting and raving, working themselves up into a frenzy, screaming until they were hoarse and tearing at their blood-stained clothes – *anything* to draw the attention of Baal!

Twelve stones

As the day drew to a close, Elijah decided that Baal had been given long enough to work up a few sparks – so he called out: 'All right. Now it's my turn. Come over here!'

The people gathered round and watched as the prophet took twelve large stones – each one repre-senting one of the twelve tribes of Israel – and rebuilt the altar of the Lord, which had been pulled down. This finished, he laid wood upon the altar and then cut up the bullock, placing the pieces on the wood.

With bated breath, the people waited for Elijah to begin praying . . . but he hadn't finished his preparations. He set to work, digging a wide trench around the altar.

When he had tossed out the last shovelful of earth, he turned to the people. 'Fill four jars with water – and pour it on the bullock and the wood.'

Water? Had the prophet forgotten there was a drought? But somehow the water was found and thrown over the altar, just as Elijah had commanded.

'Do it again,' he said. And they found more water and did it again.

'And again.' So they did it again – though they couldn't for the life of them see why. The bullock was soaked, the wood was drenched, and the trench around the altar was full to overflowing! Water was the *last* thing you put on something that you wanted to set fire to . . .

Exactly! Elijah planned to show these misguided people that God is *all-powerful*. Not only could he send fire to light the wood, but he could do it against all odds!

Bolt of fire

His preparations complete, Elijah stepped back from the altar. It was the customary time of sacrifice and

prayer. And Elijah prayed.

'Lord God of our fathers, let it be known this day that you are God of Israel, and that I am your servant, who has done all these things at your command. Hear me, O Lord, hear me, so that these people may know that you are the Lord God, and that you have drawn them back to yourself!'

The prophet hadn't even finished praying when suddenly the heavens split open and a great bolt of fire crashed down through the atmosphere and exploded on to the altar! Instantly, the bullock and the wood – and even the stones of the altar, the dust on the ground, and the water in the trench – were swallowed up in searing flames!

As one man, the people fell on their faces, crying out, 'The Lord is God! The Lord is God!'

The prophet turned and called to the people: 'Quick! The prophets of Baal are getting away! After them!'

They were all soon rounded up, and Elijah led them away to the Kishon Brook – where he executed every one of them.

Rain!

King Ahab stood watching, trembling for fear that this mighty man of God would take a sword to him too. But Elijah came to him smiling.

'Go home and organize a feast – I can hear rain coming.'

The words were music to Ahab's ears. Speechless, he turned and hurried down the mountain.

And sure enough, after Elijah had prayed – though he had to pray seven times – his assistant came to him and said: 'I saw a cloud – only a tiny one, but a cloud sure enough – rising from the sea!'

'Hurry!' said the prophet. 'Get after Ahab and tell him to make for the city at full speed – otherwise his chariot will get bogged down in the mud!'

Mud? Would there be that much rain? Oh yes – already the clouds were filling the sky, and they were blackening fast. A stiff breeze was cutting in off the sea. Soon the heavens would part – and the entire land would become a quagmire!

Oaths and curses

Yes, the storm was on its way. Meanwhile, the storm which Elijah had been sent to start had well and truly broken. Not that it would soon be over. It would take the work of another two men – the prophet Elisha and King Jehu of Israel – and a further twenty-odd years before Baal and his followers were swept from the land.

As for the 'underground church', they would do well to maintain their secrecy for a while. For when Jezebel heard that Elijah had slaughtered the prophets of Baal, venom poured from her tongue in a stream of oaths and curses.

'May the gods strike me dead,' she shrieked, 'if by this time tomorrow I haven't killed Elijah!'

And she would do the same to *any* of the Lord's people she discovered. But at least now they could rejoice in the fact that her evil days were numbered.

'God's thunderbolt' had seen to that.

Elijah/**Fact-finder**

Bible passage
You will find the story of Elijah and King Ahab in 1 Kings 16:29 – 19:2.

Time
About 860 BC. King Ahab reigned over Israel about 874 to 853 BC.

Setting of the story in history
After the reign of King David and his son, Solomon, the history of the people of Israel took a turn for the worse. The foolish oppression of the people by Solomon's son led to a revolt. Ten of the tribes making up the nation broke away to form a separate state, the northern state of Israel, with its own king. Only the tribes of Judah and Benjamin remained loyal to the kings of David's family line, who continued to rule over the tiny southern kingdom of Judah from Jerusalem.

The kings of Israel were afraid that if their people went to Jerusalem to worship God at the Temple, as they had always done, they would lose their power over them. So new places of worship were set up in Israel. This was the beginning of a growing disloyalty to God himself. Worship of pagan gods crept in, and moral standards fell. With the arrival of Jezebel as Ahab's queen, dedicated to stamping out all worship of God amongst his own people, things reached an all-time low. Into this crisis situation God sent his 'thunderbolt' – the prophet Elijah.

King Ahab
Ahab was the seventh king of Israel. His father, King Omri, a former army general, bought the commanding 300ft hill of Samaria and built a new capital there. Omri made sure that the city was well fortified. Ahab filled it with fine buildings, beginning with a magnificent palace for himself, decorated with beautiful carved ivories. Omri was a great leader, but he disobeyed God.

Ahab went even further. He married a foreign princess, Jezebel, the daughter of the king of Tyre and Sidon. And he built a temple for her god – Baal – in Samaria. Although God had forbidden his people to worship idols, Ahab worshipped Baal. And he persecuted those who were loyal to God.

Under Ahab and the kings who succeeded him, the rich got richer, and the poor more and more oppressed. Some years later, the prophet Amos had strong words to say about this injustice (read about it in the book of Amos, from 2:6 on).

You will find more about King Ahab in 1 Kings 21 – 22.

Above: *The remains of King Ahab's palace on the top of the fortified hill of Samaria.*

Many beautiful carved ivories have been found in Samaria, dating from Ahab's time. This is a typical decoration from that period.

Baal

The word 'baal' means 'lord'. The title could apply to any of the local gods of the people of Canaan. But it was used mainly for the weather god – who eventually became Baal with a capital 'b'. They prayed to Baal to make the land fertile and fruitful. They believed he controlled the weather – storms were a sign of his anger. And they tried to please him by offering sacrifices – sometimes even human ones.

Although it was forbidden in their law, the Israelites often neglected God and worshipped Baal instead. Because Baal was praised as the giver of crops, God used a drought to prove that *he* was in control of everything, from the weather to the harvest. On Mt Carmel Baal was proved absolutely powerless. It is God who is master of all things.

Above left: *Baal as weather-god, with an axe in one hand, a thunderbolt in the other.*

Above: *Just below the top of Mt Carmel is a natural amphitheatre: the sea can be seen from the top of the hill, the stream is in the valley below.*

Elijah

Elijah was the first really great prophet of Israel. The prophets were men specially chosen to declare God's message, usually in times of crisis. They were fearless in calling the king and people back to God. They reminded the people of God's standards, and his justice.

Read more about the prophet Elijah in 1 Kings 19–20, and 2 Kings 1–2. He also appears in the New Testament – see Matthew 17:1–14.

The widow who looked after Elijah during the drought would have kept oil in an earthenware cruse like the one on the right and meal or flour in a jar like the one on the left.

Places mentioned in the story
Follow the journeys on the map. From his home at Tishbe in Gilead, Elijah went to take God's message to King Ahab in Samaria, the capital city of Israel. Afterwards he crossed the River Jordan to hide near the Brook Cherith. When the brook dried up he went north to Zarephath, a city on the coast, belonging to Jezebel's father, who was king of the whole region of Tyre and Sidon.

On his way back to Samaria, Elijah met Obadiah, and arranged with King Ahab to call the people together for the great contest on Mt Carmel. When it was over, the king and the prophet went to the royal palace at Jezreel. Then Queen Jezebel's threats sent the prophet racing south for his life.

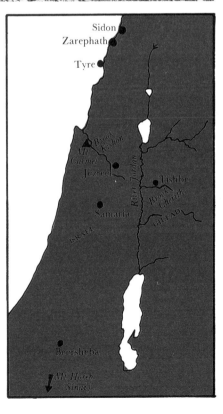

Out of the Lions' Jaws

A story of Daniel

They called it 'operation elimination' – a political plot to rid themselves of the man who prevented their promotion and dashed their plans for making extra money.

There was no doubt about it: this Daniel would have to go. It was bad enough that a foreigner should have become one of the three chief ministers of the Persian Empire. Now, it seemed, the king was planning to give him the top job. The trouble was, Daniel overshadowed the lot of them. With his superior knowledge and acute business sense, not to mention his infuriating wisdom in policy-making, he could do no wrong in the king's eyes. He was a threat to his subordinates' progress. No one else could get to the top in politics while Daniel lived.

Extermination

But to plot Daniel's extermination was easy enough; to carry it out was as big a problem as the man himself.

Naturally they couldn't afford to dirty their o[wn] hands, though each one of them would have tak[en] great pleasure in ending Daniel's life personally. V[er]bally they had stabbed him in the back more tim[es] than they could count – what they would give to [be] able to do it in actuality! But that was an idle fanc[y] the chances of being found out were far too great. Th[ey] must find a way to destroy him without harmi[ng] their own chances of succeeding to his high office.

No, something subtle was called for. A hired ass[as]sin, perhaps? But that was about as subtle as a lepe[r's] bell. Again, the risk was too high. Even if an assas[sin] were able to penetrate the wall of bodyguards w[ho] surrounded Daniel at his more vulnerable momen[ts] would he be able to deliver the fatal blow? A[nd] even if he succeeded, the odds against him escapi[ng] were far too heavy. Under interrogation he wou[ld] almost certainly break down and disclose the nam[es] of those who had hired him. The king had an excelle[nt] secret service system!

Life in danger!

Perhaps he could be poisoned . . . a few grains of so[me] deadly powder in his goblet? No way – for a m[an] of Daniel's importance had his drinks tasted for him [by] his cup-bearer. All poison would achieve would be [a] dead cup-bearer and an unmistakable announceme[nt] that Daniel's life was in danger!

Could it be that they would, after all, have to bi[de] their time and wait for fate to dismiss him from [his] earthly office? After all, Daniel was an old man surely he couldn't last much longer? But he was as [fit] and agile in body as he was in mind; who was [to] say he wouldn't outlive the very men who want[ed] him dead? This was totally unacceptable. Besid[es] they weren't prepared to wait even another wee[k] They wanted him out of the way . . . now!

Scandalous story

It annoyed them that they could not find a suitab[le] means of ending this despicable man's life. Th[ey] couldn't even bring about his downfall by spreadi[ng] some scandalous story about him, for he was *alwa[ys]* in the right! He was honest, conscientious, faithf[ul] diligent . . . and even humble; which, thought t[he] governors, was a most aggravating trait for a man [in] his position.

No, they could not find one criticism to level again[st] him. And even if they were to contrive some complain[t] and fabricate bogus evidence, the king would sure[ly] laugh at them. For Daniel, as the king was well awar[e] had proved himself faultless through many long years of royal service. He wasn't likely to start making mistakes now.

Indeed, this was one of the very reasons why they longed to be rid of him. For as First Commissioner of the Treasury, Daniel was responsible for checking and agreeing (or otherwise) the tax returns of all the king's officials. There were ways of dodging full payment – falsifying the figures – and the presidents, governors and court officials took advantage of this to boost their income. But when Daniel found out he put a stop to their fiddling. Naturally the king was pleased, for it increased his assets . . . but nobody else was smiling.

King's number one

Another grudge that was often aired when 'operation elimination' was discussed in some dark corner was the fact that this Daniel really had no right to be the king's number one – for he wasn't even a native of Persia. He was a Jew, one of many thousands taken hostage to Babylon from Jerusalem when it was conquered by King Nebuchadnezzar about seventy years earlier. He was only a lad when he left Judah, but being a prince (for he was of royal blood) he was among the young men trained and educated for service in the king's palace.

Impressed with Daniel's understanding and judgement, Nebuchadnezzar appointed him to his permanent staff of advisors . . . and from then on he took one promotion after another. Even when Babylon fell to the conquering Persians, Daniel still continued to climb the ladder of success, for every king under whom he had office admired and trusted him – and rewarded him for his service. Now he could go no higher . . . he had reached the top! And that, decided the governors, was no post for a Jew!

Strange religion

But when they examined his history in more detail, they began to realize that it was *because* he was a Jew that he had done so well. It was something to do with his God . . . yes, there was something remarkable about his strange religion. Maybe *here* they would find a loophole – a tiny breach in his 'blameless' record through which they could worm their way, undermine his integrity and bring him crashing down.

There had to be something they could latch on to; some little incident, one tiny slip . . . After all, he *was* human (although at times they almost began to question that!) and Babylon was overflowing with opportunities and enticements to indulge in human pleasures. Even the king's court had not escaped the influence of Babylon's permissive society. Why, this was 'Dazzle City' – the hub of all that was glamorous; the very fount of the glittering good life . . . surely no-one, especially a good-looking young prince, could have survived so long amidst all the temptations and delights without having stooped to savour them at some time?

But, no. His slate was clean, his copybook unblotted. As far as was humanly possible, Daniel, it appeared, was perfect. It was as though he lived on a different plane from the crowd – as though, in fact, he didn't really belong to this world at all! However could anybody exist like that? The answer again seemed to lie in his religion.

Supernatural power

The harder they searched and the deeper they dug, the more convinced they became that this was the key to his lofty living. And to his success. For they discovered that his rise to the top was studded with extraordinary displays of some sort of supernatural power – the ability to explain dreams and to interpret visions of the future. Granted, his contemporaries – the men appointed as magicians and fortune-tellers – could do very much the same, but with nowhere near the same accuracy or depth. And the one thing they certainly could not do was tell the king the nature of a dream if, when he awoke, he had forgotten it.

But Daniel could! He had, it seemed, access to the mind of his God – and with the key of prayer was able to unlock the mysteries of heaven itself. This amazed and delighted the kings – but how it frustrated and angered the astrologists!

Stronghold

The answer came to the governors quite suddenly one afternoon. If Daniel's stronghold was his religion – and it was, for he practised it so meticulously that wrongdoing couldn't even get a toe-hold in his life – then they would devise a means of making that religion itself a crime!

The word was put around, and that night 'operation

elimination' was finalized. The plot was established, examined, corrected, analysed, improved – until at last it was foolproof. It was ingenious. It couldn't fail. Daniel's fate was sealed!

The following morning the presidents and governors were granted an audience with the king.

'King Darius, live for ever!' they greeted him. 'You will be pleased to know, your Majesty, that the presidents, governors, princes, counsellors and all other officers of your kingdom have decided that there should be a law – a firm, irrevocable law – that for the next thirty days nobody should request a favour of either a god or a man, except from yourself. And that anybody who breaks this law shall be thrown to the lions.

'We request, your Majesty, that you sign the law, making it one of the special decrees of the Medes and Persians, which can never be cancelled or changed.'

The king was pleased. Making such a law appealed to him, for it put him on the level of a god. Yes,

he liked the idea immensely. How highly his governo[rs] thought of him!

'Bring me the documents,' he commanded. 'I'll sig[n] them immediately!'

Appointments with God

Of course, Daniel heard about the law even before th[e] king's seal had time to set. But he didn't panic. N[o] human legislation was going to affect his regular time[s] of communication with Almighty God. For as lon[g] as he could remember he had knelt and prayed thre[e] times each day, sharing his problems with God an[d] asking for his help. Today would be no different. H[e] would go home, throw open his bedroom window an[d] kneel down in prayer, facing Jerusalem, the ancien[t] capital city of Judah.

You could set your watch by Daniel's prayer time[s] for he was never late for his appointments with God[.] So the governors knew exactly what time to crow[d] around his house. They were confident that the[y]

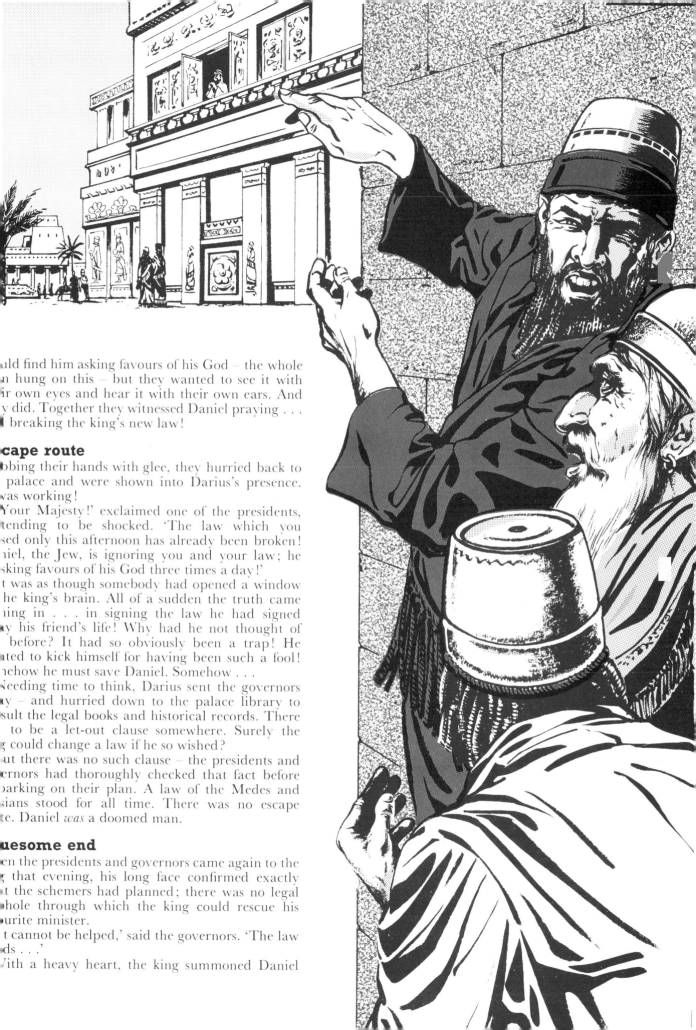

uld find him asking favours of his God – the whole
n hung on this – but they wanted to see it with
ir own eyes and hear it with their own ears. And
y did. Together they witnessed Daniel praying . . .
breaking the king's new law!

cape route

bbing their hands with glee, they hurried back to
palace and were shown into Darius's presence.
as working!

Your Majesty!' exclaimed one of the presidents,
tending to be shocked. 'The law which you
sed only this afternoon has already been broken!
niel, the Jew, is ignoring you and your law; he
sking favours of his God three times a day!'

t was as though somebody had opened a window
he king's brain. All of a sudden the truth came
ning in . . . in signing the law he had signed
y his friend's life! Why had he not thought of
before? It had so obviously been a trap! He
ted to kick himself for having been such a fool!
nehow he must save Daniel. Somehow . . .

Needing time to think, Darius sent the governors
y – and hurried down to the palace library to
sult the legal books and historical records. There
to be a let-out clause somewhere. Surely the
g could change a law if he so wished?

ut there was no such clause – the presidents and
ernors had thoroughly checked that fact before
barking on their plan. A law of the Medes and
sians stood for all time. There was no escape
te. Daniel *was* a doomed man.

uesome end

en the presidents and governors came again to the
g that evening, his long face confirmed exactly
t the schemers had planned; there was no legal
hole through which the king could rescue his
ourite minister.

t cannot be helped,' said the governors. 'The law
ds . . .'

ith a heavy heart, the king summoned Daniel

and instructed the palace guard to escort him to the lion pit. Feeling totally responsible for sending his friend to this gruesome end, the king could not bring himself to look into Daniel's eyes. Yet even in this black situation there was, the king believed, a tiny glimmer of hope.

'May your God, whom you love and serve continually, deliver you.'

Daniel said nothing.

Down in the pit the lions roared and growled. They were kept on a starvation diet so that they might quickly and eagerly devour any prisoner sentenced to their jaws. Tonight they would eat well . . . or would they?

Into the pit!

The king turned away as the guard stepped forward and pushed the prisoner down into the pit. The stone which sealed the hole was rolled into position, and the king, as was requested of him, placed his seal, and the seal of his government, upon the stone.

His eyes moist, his face flushed, Darius turned and walked quickly back to his palace. He cancelled his dinner, dismissed his entertainment, and spent the night pacing the royal bedroom, having tried – but totally failed – to escape from his conscience in sleep.

He had had restless nights before, but never a night so heart-rending – nor so long – as this. This night was a thousand years. Would it never end? Where was the dawn? Surely it should have arrived hours ago . . .

An eternity later, the first thin rays of the waking sun edged their way up from the horizon. It was morning!

Alive!

King Darius rushed out of the palace and down through the gardens to the lion pit. The law had made said the offender must be thrown to lions – nothing was mentioned about how long must remain in their company!

'Oh Daniel, servant of the living God!' cried king. 'Was your God, whom you serve continua able to deliver you from the lions?'

Was the king mad? The prisoner had been in pit for more than eight hours; the lions nee only a few minutes to strip a man to his bo Nobody went into the lions' pit and came out ali

Except Daniel . . .

'O king, live for ever!'

Darius was overwhelmed. His friend was alive!

'My God has sent his angel to shut the li mouths, so they can't hurt me! For I am inno before God, and neither have I wronged you, y Majesty.'

A bubbly mixture of joy and relief swept c King Darius as he ordered the pit to be opened Daniel lifted out. It was incredible; he was c pletely unmarked! His clothes were not torn, there wasn't so much as a scratch on his face! T man's God did wonders.

Punishment

Having seen that Daniel was fed and given a cha of clothes, King Darius ordered that the men who

duped him into signing the thirty-day law should be dragged from their beds – them and their families – and thrown to the lions. For that, thought the king, was the only punishment suitable.

There was no angel to protect anybody now. The lions pounced, and ripped the bodies apart before they'd even hit the bottom of the pit!

That very same day King Darius of Babylon made a public announcement, delivered by special messenger to everyone in his empire. It read: 'Greetings from your king. I, Darius, command that everyone everywhere shall tremble and fear before the God of Daniel. For his God is the living, unshakable God. The God whose kingdom shall never be destroyed, and whose power shall never end. He delivers and rescues his people, working great miracles in heaven and earth – for it is he who delivered Daniel from the jaws of the lions!'

The total weight of the Persian government had been behind the plot to eliminate Daniel. You'd have thought that with all their know-how and cunning they would have been more than a match for one old man. But they had failed to consider that old man's God – and the job which God had given him to do. For in the darkness of the heathen courts of Babylon Daniel was like a candle shining out for God. The winds of persecution and hatred blew their hardest; but not even a gale could have snuffed out *God's* candle . . .

He had his hand around the flame.

Daniel/**Fact-finder**

Bible passage

You will find this story in Daniel 6. The story of Daniel's earlier life at court in Babylon is told in Daniel 1 – 5. The rest of the book of Daniel describes his visions in exile, many about future events.

Time

We can't be sure about this. It depends whether Darius in this story is Darius I (who reigned 522–486) or someone else (perhaps Cyrus himself). We know that Daniel was taken to Babylon in 605 and that by the time of this story he was an old man.

Setting of the story in history

This story belongs to the end of the Old Testament history of Israel – only Ezra, Esther and Nehemiah are later. (Read the Fact-finder pages of the Nehemiah story to discover what happened from the time of King David to the time of the exile.)

Daniel arrived in Babylon as a boy. He belonged to one of the leading families in Jerusalem. But the Babylonian army hammered at the city gates. They did not trust King Jehoiakim and they demanded hostages to take to Babylon, to make sure he kept the peace. So Daniel, his three friends, and many others made the 700-mile journey to the capital of

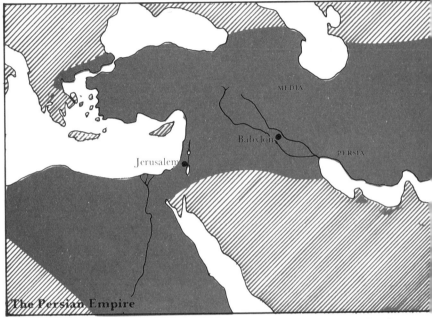

The Persian Empire

the great Babylonian Empire, where King Nebuchadnezzar had just begun his long and glorious reign. You will find more about this in the story of the fiery furnace, in *Great Adventures of the Bible*.

Daniel outlived King Nebuchadnezzar. He outlived Belshazzar. He lived to see the Medes and Persians defeat the Babylonians and take over the city. The kings came and went, but Daniel remained in high office. And his character was unchanged, too. From boyhood to old age, Daniel was true to the God he had learned to love and worship in

far-off Jerusalem. Every day he prayed, kneeling at his open window looking west over the city buildings t the flat fields of the plain beyond (an in his mind's eye seeing Jerusalem and God's holy Temple). Everyone knew about this – and that was how his enemies hoped to trap him . . .

The Persian Empire

When Cyrus the Persian defeated the armies of Babylon and brought the Babylonian Empire to an end, he did not destroy the capital. The citizens, in great relief, welcomed him – and h treated them well. Babylon remained the glorious city it had been under King Nebuchadnezzar. The great walls and broad streets, fine building and temples remained.

Cyrus was a man of unusual tolerance. He allowed the peoples he conquered to worship their own god He even granted funds for this. And so it was in character when he allowe the Jews to go home to Jerusalem,

The 9 inch clay cylinder which records King Cyrus' capture of Babylon without a battle.

A lion of glazed tile which decorated the Processional Way in Babylon.

taking with them the spoil the Babylonians had taken from the Temple. God's promise that his people would return from exile was fulfilled at last.

The Persian Empire was far greater than the Empires of Assyria and Babylonia. It extended from the Indus river across modern Iran, Iraq and Turkey to the Aegean Sea, and south into Egypt. Cyrus was a first-rate administrator, organizing his territory under satraps (governors) and army commanders, establishing a code of laws, and a postal system throughout the Empire. He allowed subject peoples a good deal of freedom to see to their own affairs under the general oversight of his officers. And the result was peace and stability.

King Darius I in his chariot, hunting lions.

This modest building marks the grave of Cyrus the Great in the palace of Parsagarda, near Persepolis in Persia. It is empty now, but these are the words once inscribed above the door: 'O man, whoever you are and whenever you come, for I know that you will come – I am Cyrus, who gave the Persians their empire. Do not grudge me this patch of earth that covers my body.'

The lion-pit

The lion was regarded as a symbol of royalty, and many of the kings of Assyria and Babylonia kept and bred lions in captivity. Lion hunting was the sport of Assyrian kings, and is pictured in stone relief in their palaces at Nineveh, about 100 years before this story. Darius's lion-pit was probably an enclosure with an open top and a small entrance at the side which the king sealed up.

Project Jerusalem

The story of Nehemiah

It was the trumpet you had to listen for. That was the alarm signal. When we heard it we dropped our tools, grabbed our swords, and raced around or through the city to where Nehemiah stood facing the enemy. There we would fall into our battle ranks, ready for action.

Not that I ever crossed swords with any Samaritans myself; there were one or two minor skirmishes, of course, but for most of the time it was a case of just baring our teeth and looking mean – showing them that we meant business; that we were ready to defend Jerusalem with our lives.

Thinking back on it, though, I realize that it was God's goodness and not our defiant defence programme which kept us out of trouble. At the time we may have kidded ourselves that we were more than a match for them – but the truth is·that the enemy far outnumbered us. And on top of that we were the most unlikely-looking army that ever drew swords – having come straight from the building site. It must have been difficult to tell whether we were sword-waving labourers or chisel-packing soldiers!

The fact is, we were both.

Mockery and scorn

We'd come to do a job – originally to rebuild the Temple of Jerusalem, and later the city walls – and we were going to see it through. But from the moment our families had arrived back in Judah, our homeland, we were the subject of mockery and scorn – and not a few attempts were made to scare us off.

Nehemiah, who had been appointed governor of Jerusalem and chief engineer, ordered that the city be guarded day and night. Further, every man had to be ready to fight at a moment's notice, which meant working with our swords strapped to our sides and our shields and mail-coats close at hand. When things got really rough, and it looked as though the enemy might be on our backs any minute, only half the men worked while the other half stood guard behind them.

Now you might ask, why go to all this trouble just to build a place where we could live and worship? Was it really worth all the blisters and backache, not to mention the chance of getting our throats cut by an enemy raiding party? After all, there were other more friendly places to live – and there must have been towns and cities that needed no more than repair and renovation to make them habitable. Jerusalem was literally a pile of rubble. It needed complete rebuilding.

I'll admit it sounds a crazy place to choose. But, you see, we hadn't returned to Jerusalem simply to reconstruct our homes . . . We were there to rebuild the Jewish nation.

I'd better explain . . .

Invading forces

About a hundred and fifty years earlier the city of Jerusalem had been utterly destroyed. And the Jewish people (they were called Israelites then) were dragged off by the invading forces of Babylon. They left a few peasant farmers behind, but by and large the entire Jewish nation was deported seven hundred miles away to Babylonia. The great name of Israel was no more.

Where was the mighty God who had delivered his people from their enemies on so many previous occasions? He had abandoned them! And it wasn't surprising, for they just would not be true to him. I expect you've heard of all the times God warned them, punished them, forgave them and restored them as a nation. But now they had gone too far; they had tried God's patience one time too many – so he tossed them aside into the iron grip of their enemies.

But God is good. He didn't abandon them for ever. He still intended to show to the world through the Jews that he is the only true God. While our forefathers were imprisoned in Babylon, he declared that after seventy years his people would be released – and they were, when Babylon was conquered by Cyrus, king of Persia.

Special responsibility

God put it into Cyrus's heart to be kind to our people. He allowed us to return home so that we could rebuild the Temple at Jerusalem. Apparently the king felt that God had given him this task as a special responsibility. I'm sorry to say that a lot of Jewish families decided to stay in Babylon, having already started to set up home, raise their families and settle into steady jobs. I can understand that. After all, they knew that if they left for Jerusalem they would have to spend four months trekking across the desert. And when they got there they would be exchanging their comfortable homes and secure jobs for a tumble-down city, hostile neighbours, and hard, dirty work. Nobody held it against them for staying. I think they knew that they ought to have gone. But when you're comfortable it's difficult to dig up your roots and follow your convictions.

However, those who really loved our God and wanted to rebuild his Temple and re-establish the

respect of the Jewish nation, accepted Cyrus's invitation and set out for the old capital.

Old enemies

About fifty thousand Jews, my family among them, came down in that great exodus. My grandfather was only a boy when he left Babylon. He told me that they came in fear and trembling, for they were coming back to a land which had been overrun by Israel's old enemies. It was nothing short of suicidal. Yet they had faith that God would not be thwarted; that his plans would be realized, even though the once vast, powerful nation of Israel had now been whittled down to a few thousand timid, faltering believers.

Once they reached the city, though, they put their fears aside and got stuck into their work. Then the opposition brought it all to a standstill for fifteen years. But eventually building began again, and in four years the new Temple was completed and dedicated. Agreed, it wasn't anywhere near as splendid as Solomon's Temple – but it was the best that could be built with the materials and manpower available, and that was all God asked.

Having completed the Temple, however, our people were oppressed and intimidated more and more by the neighbouring nations. In the end it became impossible to carry on with any further building in safety. So work stopped for about eighty years. It seemed as if dream of making the name of Israel great again was *only* a dream. And it would remain a dream – unless we could find a leader; somebody to take control, to organize the people into a team again; somebody who, fired with dedication to this great cause, could rekindle the flame of determination in the hearts of the nation.

But only God could send such a man. And the ma he sent, as I expect you've gathered, was Nehemia

Hungry for news

Nehemiah was the king's cup-bearer at the court Artaxerxes, fourth king of Persia after Cyrus. Being Jew, he was always hungry for news of the settleme in Jerusalem. And when he learned from his ov brother that the walls were still in ruins and the gat urned and broken, he sat down and cried. And as e cried, he prayed that God would move the king o relieve him of his duty so that he could go to erusalem and undertake the rebuilding of the city.

Four months later Nehemiah was on his way. Not nly had the king granted him leave, but he had anded him documents instructing the manager of the orest to give him a consignment of timber to help n the construction work.

But it wasn't all good news. Two of our arch-nemies – Tobiah, an Ammonite, and Sanballat, a Horonite – heard of Nehemiah's arrival under escort rom the king of Persia's royal guard, and were furious hat anyone should try to help us. They didn't yet know what Nehemiah's mission was. But from the moment hey clapped eyes on him they determined to prevent him from carrying it out.

Troublemakers

Sensing that he was being watched, Nehemiah waited hree days before attempting any sort of appraisal of he work that needed to be done. And even then he carried out his inspection of the ruins under cover of darkness.

When he had completed his initial survey, he gathered us together and shared with us his findings – and his vision.

'You know only too well the terrible state of the city,' he said. 'It lies in ruins! So let's rebuild the wall – and banish this disgrace!'

We didn't need any prompting. This man's con-viction was infectious – and the response unanimous.

We *would* rebuild the wall!

Obviously you can't keep a project of this scale secret. The moment we began clearing away the rubble and picking out the usable stones, word of our intentions spread. We hadn't been working for more than a few hours when the troublemakers appeared. Sanballat and Tobiah, together with Geshem the Arab, came riding up to Nehemiah.

'What do you think you're doing?' they roared. 'This is nothing short of rebellion! The king won't stand for it!'

But Nehemiah coolly turned, looked them in the eye, and said: 'The God of heaven will see this through! We're his servants, and we're going to build this wall!'

Petty abuse

It seemed that these three rogues had nothing better to do with their time than to plague us with their insults. When they saw that the building was going well, they came by with a bunch of their unsavoury friends. For a few minutes they laughed and shouted out petty abuse. But then Sanballat became angry. He stamped his foot and bawled out: 'Look at these feeble Jews! Are they trying to build a fortress? It'll

take you more than a day! You'd better offer some more sacrifices! Hah, look at the rubbishy old stones they're using! Fancy digging them out of the rubble and using them again!'

Then Tobiah chipped in: 'Call it a wall! Why, if even a fox skipped along the top of it, it would collapse into dust again!'

We turned to Nehemiah. We couldn't answer these scoffers, and apparently he wouldn't. He was gazing up to heaven, praying.

'O Lord God, hear us. You see that we are hated and mocked. May their insults rebound on their own heads, and may they themselves be taken captive into a foreign land. For in despising those who build your wall, they are despising you!'

When they realized that their scoffing was cutting no ice, they shut up and rode off. But I was troubled by something Sanballat had said: 'Are they trying to build a fortress?' Could this be what lay behind their efforts to discourage us? Were they frightened that we *would* build a fortress – a stronghold from which we would ride out to attack them and plunder their cities?

The history books are packed with stories of how our ancestors were a mighty, warring people who came into Canaan and took possession, grinding their enemies into the dirt beneath their feet. Sanballat and his friends were afraid the same would happen again!

I became convinced of this when, once we had built up the wall to half its original height, they plotted to lead an army against the city. The time for

derision was over. If they couldn't dissuade us by hurling insults, they would try to stop us by hurling spears.

Prayer and action

Nehemiah was a very practical man. He didn't believe that every battle could be won on his knees. When prayer was called for, he prayed. But when action was needed, he got on and did whatever had to be done. The threat of attack was real enough. So work on the wall was temporarily suspended while we prepared for the enemy. We had word that they were planning to charge us . . . that they intended to take us by surprise, and kill us. So we prepared ourselves. But Nehemiah saw that we were troubled, and called us together to pray with him. Then he encouraged us: 'Don't be afraid. Remember that the Lord is great and powerful. Fight for your families, your friends and your homes!'

As it turned out, we didn't even have to dirty our swords. When our enemies realized that we knew of their plans, and that we were ready for them, they turned back, frustrated and furious. I gather they spent the rest of the day trying to find out who had leaked their plans to us. But they never found him.

Constant vigil

So we went back to work. But, as I was telling you earlier, we could no longer throw our entire energies into the building programme. It was a case of keeping a constant vigil and, as I said, listening out for that trumpet. Nehemiah was convinced that the danger wasn't over yet. The moment we dropped our guard, he told us, they'd be on us.

As a result we had to tighten up security all round. Those of us who had been living outside the city had to move inside, and from that day on till we finished the work we never took off our clothes, nor went anywhere without our weapons.

These measures seemed to be effective – but Sanballat and Tobiah hadn't given up yet. One day a

message arrived for Nehemiah, inviting him to meet them for a chat in a village on the Plain of Ono. But we all saw right through their ruse. It was a plot to kill our great governor. They reasoned, and rightly, that with Nehemiah out of the way we would panic and scatter like chickens before a fox. So Nehemiah sent them this reply: 'I am doing a great work here. Why should I stop just to make small talk with you?'

Accusations

Four times the tricksters sent the same invitation – and four times they got the same reply. Finally they sent a letter loaded with accusations against us, and designed to force Nehemiah into meeting them – and stepping into their trap.

This letter confirmed my earlier suspicions. It read: 'Our friend Geshem says there are rumours throughout the country that the Jews are planning to rise up against their neighbours. That is why you are building the wall. The rumours say that you plan to be king of the Jews, and that you have employed men to promote your name so that the people of Judah will rally to Jerusalem and join your rebellious band.

'You can be sure that the king of Persia will hear of this – unless, of course, you meet us so that we can talk it over.'

But Nehemiah didn't waste any words on them.

His reply, which I personally carried to Tobiah, simply stated: 'You're a pack of liars! You've invented this story to try to scare us into stopping work!'

Message from God

Sanballat and Tobiah's last attempt to snare Nehemiah almost fooled him, I suppose because he didn't think they would stoop so low.

He had gone to see Shemaiah, one of the prophets, who said that he had received a message from God.

'Let's hide in the Temple,' he urged Nehemiah, 'for your enemies are coming to kill you tonight!'

Nehemiah was shocked. 'What! Should the governor of Jerusalem run from danger? Besides, I'm not a priest – if I hide in the Temple I wouldn't save my life, I'd lose it!'

Nehemiah told us later that as soon as he said this, he realized it was a subtle trap. God hadn't spoken to Shemaiah! The man was in the pay of Sanballat and Tobiah! They had persuaded him to scare Nehemiah into running from their threats. Had they succeeded he would have lost his credibility as governor of the city – and the work would have collapsed . . . the wall would never have been finished.

Miracle!

But, thanks to our wonderful God, and his wise servant, the wall *was* finished, and in record time. It took just fifty-two days, and that was nothing short of a miracle!

Just as miraculous, though it took a lot longer, was the reconstruction of the Jewish nation. It began when God allowed our people to be carried off into Babylon – for there he finally cured us of idol-worship. And it was brought to completion because a cup-bearer in the king's palace threw up his life of luxury, ease and security . . . and got his hands dirty for God.

Nehemiah/**Fact-finder**

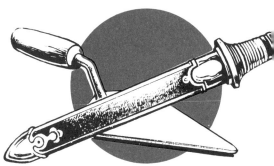

Bible passage
You will find this story in Nehemiah 1–6. The rest of the book of Nehemiah tells what happened after the walls were built, how Nehemiah governed and reformed the nation.

Time
The building of the wall took place about 445 BC.

Setting of the story in history
The story of Nehemiah comes late in the Old Testament history of Israel. The days of the kings – the united kingdom of David and Solomon; the divided kingdoms of Israel and Judah after Solomon's death – are long past.

First the northern kingdom fell to the Assyrians. Samaria, the capital, fell in 722 – and Israel ceased to exist. Jerusalem had a narrow escape soon after, when the Assyrian King Sennacherib attacked, but survived – only to fall in turn to the Babylonians under Nebuchadnezzar in 587. Many of the people were taken away captive to Babylonia. This was God's punishment on the nation for disobeying his laws and worshipping heathen idols.

There they stayed in exile until Cyrus the Persian swept away the Babylonian Empire in 539, and allowed the captives to return to their homelands. Some of the Jews were ready and waiting. (They were called Jews by this time, for these were the people from the southern kingdom, Judah.) God had told them through the prophets – Isaiah and Jeremiah and the visionary Ezekiel – that all this would happen. He had promised to take them home and build a new nation out of those who remained faithful to him.

Others had put down roots in Babylon. They were not prepared to leave behind the civilized comforts they had worked so hard for. The prospect of beginning again in the ruins of Jerusalem did not appeal. So they stayed.

But large numbers of Jews faced the dangers and hardships of the long journey and returned, with Zerubbabel as their leader (about 538). More went later with Ezra (about 458). They met all kinds of problems. The people who had settled in the land while they were away were afraid of them and made trouble. But they managed to rebuild the Temple – just a modest one, not at all the grand affair that Solomon had built. Jerusalem was God's city again.

But the city still had no walls. It was defenceless. And at last Nehemiah in the king's court away in Babylon heard the sad news that made him decide that something must be done . . .

When the Assyrians and Babylonians captured and plundered a city, they often deported the people and resettled the land with foreigners. Here the people are leaving the captured city in ox-carts with their sheep and cattle, while Assyrian scribes stand by, recording the spoil.

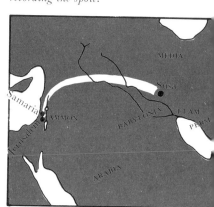

Places mentioned in the story
Nehemiah was at Susa, the Persian King Artaxerxes' winter capital, whe he heard the sad news from Jerusalem. It was a journey of about 800 miles across rivers and desert and mountain to his homeland. But the whole area – from the Persian Gulf to the Mediterranean and south into Egypt – was under the Persian king's control, and he was able to arrange safe-conduct.

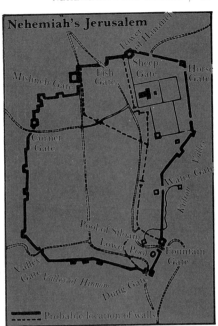

This picture of the wall of the Temple area in Jerusalem today shows the strength of city walls. Some of these stones were put in position as long ago as Nehemiah's time.

The king's cup-bearer

Nehemiah was not just a minor palace servant. The king trusted him with his life. For it was Nehemiah's job to see that the king's wine was not poisoned. From very early times the position of cup-bearer to the king was an important and influential one, and much sought-after. Few people were closer to the king, saw him more often, shared more of his confidences. And this often meant political power.

From the story it is clear that Nehemiah was a man of outstanding ability – a leader and organizer of men, who expected and got high standards and loyal obedience from those under him.

The city walls

In Old Testament times cities were built, not primarily for people to live in, but for defence. They were fortresses, to take in people from the surrounding country in time of war. The site was chosen with this in mind. And strong walls were the most important factor in the city's defence, once they had made sure of a water supply that would outlast a siege.

From a sloping base of earth and great stones, sheer stone walls topped with sun-baked brick 10 or 12ft thick rose 25 to 30ft high. The walls were strengthened with towers, which gave the defenders a good vantage-point for hurling missiles at the enemy. Sometimes the city was protected by a double wall. Smaller cities had a single gate, flanked with towers. Larger ones – like Nehemiah's Jerusalem – had several narrow gates as well as the main one.

As time went on and the cities had to survive the attack of battering-rams and siege-engines (which brought the enemy bowmen level with the defenders on the walls), they had to build higher and stronger still. Soon after Nehemiah's day solid stone walls were normal. Some of the stones in the Temple wall built by Herod the Great, at the time of Jesus, were 22ft long!

The walls of Jerusalem had been broken down by the Babylonians when they captured the city in 587 BC. The buildings were set on fire. And the local limestone used for the walls crumbled in the blaze. For 140 years the walls were left to the erosion of wind and weather. And the people who settled the land no doubt made use of the stone for their own buildings. So Nehemiah's task was daunting, to say the least. He needed his strong faith in God, as well as great determination, to carry it out. But in 52 days of non-stop work, with everyone on the job, the walls were finished. Jerusalem was a city again. The disgrace of her destruction was wiped away.

A battering-ram being used to break into a walled city. The metal-tipped rams are operated by soldiers hidden inside the machine. The whole is covered with leather strengthened with metal discs.